JACK DAVIS

The Maker of History

Edited by Gerry Turcotte

ETT IMPRINT

Exile Bay

First published by ETT Imprint, Exile Bay 2023

First published by Angus & Robertson 1994

ETT IMPRINT
PO Box R1906
Royal Exchange NSW 1225
Australia

ISBN 978-1-923024-34-2 (paper)
ISBN 978-1-923024-35-9 (ebook)

Design by Tom Thompson

Cover: Jack Davis

To the memory of
Oodgeroo Noonuccal

CONTENTS

'The Maker of History': Jack Davis - An Introduction

GERRY TURCOTTE

I first met Jack Davis in 1989. I was running a writing series at the University of Sydney and had had him flown over from Perth as a guest of the programme. He had just published *Barungin (Smell the Wind)*, and, the attention generated both from the subject of deaths in custody as well as from the play based on and exposing that subject, had put Jack Davis even more in the spotlight than usual. Even so, I was surprised by what happened soon after he stepped off the plane.

I knew what he looked like, of course, from the many photographs I had studied and from the various televised interviews I had seen. And when his familiar hat emerged above the crowd I made my way towards him and introduced myself. But before we had taken a dozen steps the words 'Uncle Jack' rose up from all around us. There was a blur of movement, and soon we were surrounded by a group of Aboriginal youths who milled around Jack, not so much the way people swarm a rock star, but rather the way one greets a favourite family member.

And for what seemed a long time he shook hands, hugged, kissed and was immersed entirely in this reunion where names and places were exchanged. Then we left the group and made our way into the city.

To me the encounter had a touch of magic to it, but clearly for Jack this was a usual though no less special event. No, he didn't know anyone in particular; but they were related, he said, they knew him through his work, his place in the community - his words. And he, quite obviously, knew them; their stories, their lineage.

This moment was special in its own way in that it suggested the power, A vision and reach of Jack Davis, the writer, the political figure and the person. It was a visible index of the effect he has had in the community at large, a community which, because of his skill, has extended far beyond the parameters of the Aboriginal one.

Certainly this reach is a refutation of those critics who would seek to limit his appeal exclusively to either a white or a black audience. Clearly he speaks for the Aboriginal population of Australia; but his success as a playwright throughout the world, and his reception by both indigenous and non-indigenous peoples from Canada to Australia, suggest that Davis has succeeded in tapping into a vein that threads across generations, language barriers and of course racial lines.

We are all wary of the fiction of universalism and it is not my intention here to blithely use the label. Nor is it my aim to vitiate the very special racial focus of Davis's work by claiming (and perhaps thus appropriating) it for a white, or even an academic, audience. I do think it is fair to say, however, that part of Davis's 'purpose' in writing is both to celebrate the Aboriginal voices of Australia, and to raise them loudly in areas which for so long seemed deaf to their words.

It would also be fair to say that this country's hearing has improved greatly. In Australia, and in fact around the world, there has been an explosion of work by and about indigenous writers, and this volume is part of that growing interest and celebration. The fact that it was 'assembled' in the Year of the Indigenous Peoples is a further happy accident.

In spite (or perhaps in view) of this 'improving' social climate, Jack Davis's work has to be given credit for shaping that creative space in some large measure, and the articles in this volume suggest to what extent his influence is to be credited. I have invited a number of people - long familiar with both Davis's *oeuvre* and the man himself - to speak with or reread his contribution to Australian letters.

In 'The Real Australian Story', Adam Shoemaker continues what is in effect a long dialogue with the writer, one which has seen the two work together on a number of projects including the co-editing (with Mudrooroo Narogin and Stephen Muecke) of a now well-known anthology (*Paperbark*). Perhaps most exciting about this interview is that it is possible for Davis to stand back and assess the great changes which have taken place over the last ten years in the Australian racial and literary landscape - and to welcome a 'blossoming in the field' of black Australian literature, as Shoemaker puts it.

Asked to predict what the following decade will offer for Aboriginal people, Davis suggests that, 'As far as writers are concerned, I think the future looks good for them. I think it'll be good for stage and good for film. As for Aboriginal people - politically - I don't think we're going to get very far ...' It will be interesting to see whether his predictions for the future will be as accurate as those of the previous decade. It is to be hoped that Davis is wrong in his pessimism about change.

Certainly the political landscape of Australia is slow to transform. It was only recently, for example, that Terra Nullius was finally abolished from Australia's legal framework, a doctrine which had the effrontery to say that Australia was 'a land belonging to no one' when the European settlers first arrived here. It was a policy that allowed for wholesale dispossession of land and rights, one which has continued to work against the Aboriginal peoples in today's courts of law. And yet, despite this reluctance to change, Australia has transformed itself, and two figures stand out as major catalysts. One, we know, is Davis. The other is the late Oodgeroo Noonuccal. A long-time friend of Davis, a poet, an artist and a tireless political activist, it was absolutely imperative in my eyes that her voice be joined to those in this volume.

When I spoke to Oodgeroo, I asked her to put together a biographical sketch of Davis's career. Not surprisingly, what she provided was inextricably linked to a reading of his poetry, a reading which is political and personal at the same time. This connection is perhaps inevitable. As Oodgeroo has herself argued elsewhere, 'If you talk about a hole in the street up there that's politics. And this old cliched business of saying we are non-political. If you're non-political, man, you're dead, you're not even thinking.'! Or, as Davis himself puts it in the Shoemaker interview, 'if you're Aboriginal then you're a politician. If you're black, you're political.'[1]

Oodgeroo's tribute charts Davis's work from the beginning of the 1960s, and situates many of his poems, plays and performances in their political context. In this way we are offered a unique insight into the production process of one of this country's most celebrated writers.

'To My Brother Jack Davis' captures both the frustra¬tion of dealing with a recalcitrant white world-'He came to the conclusion that he and I were either very bad educators or that our good "Gubbariginals" (white friends) were slow learners' - as well as the euphoria of successfully reaching an audience - 'He is known all over the world for he has travelled much to introduce audiences of all races to his plays, poems and writings'. She concludes, 'To me, he will always be a cherished brother and valued friend who will be' remembered as one of the greatest artists, writers, poets and humanitarians that Australia and our Earth Mother have had the wisdom to birth'. These are words which apply equally to

Oodgeroo. Her contribution here, therefore, her last formal project, has particular resonance.

When we talk about Jack Davis's critical reputation, it would be difficult to ignore the fact that it is based largely on his plays. In 'Oral Culture, Theatre, Text', Joanne Tompkins provides a reading of Davis's plays which emphasises the extent to which he has forced a reassessment of Australian history and Australian drama, largely through his fusion - or hybridizing - of Aboriginal oral culture and Western dramatic forms. It is an 'intersection' which means that 'Aboriginal drama must be watched and read differently from white drama'. It is this connection to oral culture.ithen, which is the distinguishing feature of Davis's drama and the focus of Tompkins's chapter.

Davis is a master of statement through juxtaposition of white versus black custom, of traditional versus urban Aboriginal life, and so forth. In Kullark he uses the device of the screen backdrop, painted with Aboriginal and British icons. Throughout the play the British images truncate the Dreamtime Serpent, metaphorically suggesting the increasing incursion by whites into the Aboriginal experience.

Davis also uses his texts to highlight or expose cultural practices which are taken for granted. In the still unpublished Wahngin Country, Davis creates a naive, or innocent, character and uses him to comment on what is considered by whites to be a typical or 'normal' social institution - Christianity. The protagonist of Wahngin Country tells of one of his friends who entered St Mary's Cathedral only to decide, after the service, that the church was 'a bloody casino'.

When asked how he knew this, Ernie explained:

'Well one bloke standin' up the front all dressed up with red clothes on, and these little boys with red and white clothes on. And the big watjella in the red clothes sings

out dominos robiscum, and the watjellas sing out et cum
spirit toto.' 'Jesus Christ' says Mick 'what that mean?'
'My father can play dominoes better than your father can
and them watjellas are saying ''pigs arse he can,''and it's a
casino alright, cause there's these two blokes walkin' down
the aisle takin' side bets.' [2]

In a wonderfully comic moment, Davis illustrates how much white culture normalises its own customs; and by shifting the point of view in this way he shows that these practices are far from neutral. The reader becomes conscious of the value-laden nature of such terms, practices and institutions, and is made aware of how all such rituals are culturally relative.

In In *Our Town* Davis extends this comment on Christianity in a harsher way. Old Uncle Herbie, who has been setting rabbit traps on a local farmer's property, cannot understand why his snares are constantly being torn down and he himself threatened with arrest. At one stage he says to Joe, 'Mr Crawford and his missus, they go to church every Sunday, then he come home and knock my snares down. Christians!'[3] What so confuses Uncle Herbie, of course, is that the land he is hunting on is Aboriginal land.

It is a moment which reminds us of a scene in *Kullark* where Yagan is similarly confused over the fact that whites can kill kangaroos, duck, swan and mullet at will, but shoot Aborigines for helping themselves to the imported sheep. When the' sympathetic settler, Will, tries to explain ('the sheep belong to the white man ... But all those [other] things belong to everyone'), who can fail to sympathise with Yagan's passionate response: 'Archh, *Wetjala kartwarrah'*[4] [" ... white man is mad"]'." Through deceptively simple juxtapositions such as these, Davis succeeds in highlighting the extraordinary inequities which have characterised black and white relations, but reverses the general impression (advanced in classroom history texts for over two hundred years) that it was indigenous behaviour that defied reason.

Song, dance and even opposing constructions of. history also serve to foreground difference. The very 'absence' of Aboriginal culture from contemporary institutions has often been seen as a proof of its insignificance. But, as Tompkins points out, what Davis's plays do is 'express the validity of Aboriginal history and forms', making clear that this 'void' is merely a white construction.

It is also important to recognise that Davis's drama does not argue for a return to pre-contact experience. The plays acknowledge the inevitability of interaction, and argue instead for a revitalised understanding of hybridity rather than a reactionary vision of assimilation.

This argument for hybridization - displayed at the level of both theme and form - suggests the potential for Aboriginal culture to enrich and modify white experience, rather than painting the more usual picture of Aboriginal culture being subsumed and ultimately destroyed by the majority culture.

If Davis's plays have introduced important formal innovations that have challenged European literary conceits, it is just as true that his work has had an impact reshaping the very stage on which such dramas are enacted. Helen Gilbert's paper '"Talking Country": Place and *Dis*placement in Jack Davis's Theatre' examines the way that Davis's plays deal with the subject of space itself - in particular, with the relationship between place, history and Aboriginality. Since the history of Aborigines in Australia is in effect a story of *dis*placement, Gilbert argues that it is appropriate to read the plays in terms of the way they reclaim, and even reconceptualise, 'place and space so that the legitimacy of white settlement is undermined'.

Gilbert rightly argues that in performance genres, 'narratives unfold in space as well as through time', and drama therefore allows a 'simultaneous reading ... of all the visual and aural signifiers embedded in the text as performance'. In Davis's plays the stage itself is a politicised landscape, a contested ground upon which ideas, values and politics are represented or negotiated. It is for this reason that Davis's restructuring of that space is significant. In some productions of *No Sugar*, for example, the audience was forced to follow the players, duplicating in a minor way the dispossession of the figures in the play. In In *Our Town* a line divides the stage, and rarely do white and black characters cross that barrier. And, as Gilbert points out, in *Wahngin Country* 'Davis's contemporary Aboriginal protagonist continues the search for an empowering space from which to speak' as he performs, promenade-style, moving from a traditional campsite to an urban park bench while the audience follows'. The title of the play translates as 'Talking Country', and, as Gilbert suggests, the title and its particular form assert 'the links between the land and the articulation of Aboriginal identities'.

Theatre, from the time of the Greeks to the present day, has often been a forum for expressing the majority view. Davis joins a long line of 'interlopers' who invade and conquer this space. I am reminded of a story Davis himself told me of the performance of *No Sugar* in Vancouver. Native people, he said, largely unable to pay the entrance fee to see his play, were let in through the exits by the Aboriginal actors. It was a collusion that physically enacted the 'message' of the play about reclaiming or reappropriating the speaking places.

If Jack Davis is Australia's best-known Aboriginal playwright, then no doubt Ernie Dingo is its most famous actor. It is fitting, then, to discover that the latter got his start in theatre through Davis's plays. In 'Breaking the Rules of Theatre', we are offered a glimpse of the evolution of Davis's skills in the theatre, but from a perspective which makes it clear both how powerful the work can be on an imaginative and social scale, and how significant Davis's work has been on a personal scale, giving purpose and direction to Aboriginal observers, from actors to audiences. As Dingo puts it, 'I along with other fortunate Aboriginal actors was lucky to be able to start in theatre with JD . . . And we were proud to know that no theatre training school in Australia, could teach us to act like the Aboriginals that he wanted us to be. Proud, upstanding and family. Together.'

Significantly, Dingo, like Tompkins, underscores the fact that a large part of Davis's impact was achieved not by bending his will to white theatrical expectations, but rather by refusing t9 give in to these 'rules of theatre'. 'We believed in what we were doing', Dingo points out, 'we just did it in a different way. There was no thought to degrade our Aboriginality, our writers or ourselves ... Uncle Jack would break the rules.'

I suggested earlier that Davis's fame rests largely on his theatrical work, and though this is true, it is also a fact that his poetry has been unfairly neglected, or, worse, frequently' dismissed. David Headon's article, 'Spanning the Sky with Outstretched Hands', will do much to restore this work to its proper place within the writer's body of work and more widely in the Aboriginal and the white Australian poetic canons.

Headon correctly points out that part of this vilification is because of Davis's reliance on European traditions or forms in his poetry. This reliance is due in some part to his own upbringing, to his preferred poetic models and even to his desire to keep his poems accessible. But beyond this, Davis's work also puts the lie to many of his critics' harshest accusations - criticisms which suggest that his work is 'soft', insufficiently 'political' or more pointedly, that it is '*un*Aboriginal'.

Ironically, indigenous writers have frequently complained that they resent the expectation which attaches itself to their writing: that because they are Aboriginal they must write on a specific theme or in a specific form. Native writer and critic, Thomas King, argues that indigenous writers are not 'given the same latitude' as non-Aboriginal writers. They are expected to write like Indians, or Aborigines, solely about indigenous issues. And yet, as he points out, 'we need to be reminded that while literature can be a great many things, we should not insist that it be a proper cultural catechism as well'.[5]

To argue that indigenous writers need not be tied to specific issues is not to say that their work cannot be political or even culturally specific. Headon, of course, makes it quite clear that, far from being unpolitical, Davis's 'verse of the last two decades points to a poet who has worked hard at his craft both for love and for the political opportunities the genre can provide'. Moreover, there is a marked evolution throughout the four volumes of poetry which shows Davis becoming increasingly optimistic about the survival - perhaps even the renaissance - of Aboriginal culture.

No Sugar makes this point most clearly. The play opens in 1929. The Millimurra household is alive with activity and contradiction. According to the stage directions, for example, the children play cricket (which is an imported British game) while Jimmy sharpens an axe (bush style). Joe Millimurra is reading the special centenary edition of the *Western Mail*, a newspaper which here represents the voice of white society - the voice of power - and the lead story is about the celebration of that coming to power. The article which Joe is reading aloud, it could be argued, is a metaphor for the way white history is oblivious to black reality and experience. It is the 'Official Document' of history which, since settlement, has been the only voice heard in Australia.

But in the opening of *No Sugar*, this official history is constantly edited and interrupted by black voices that question the truth of what we hear. The first thing Joe reads is that there has been a recreation of the early days of the pioneers, which features three lorries filled with Aborigines. These actors represent the threat that faced the 'brave pioneers' in their attempt to claim Australia for God and King.

When Joe reads that the pageant 'presented a picture of Western Australia's present condition of hopeful optimum-optimis-tic prosperity', Sam answers, 'Sounds like bullshit to me'. And in reference to the Aborigines dancing in the parade, Sam says, 'Nyoongahs corroboreein' to a *wetjalas'* brass band!' to which Jimmy adds, 'That beats every thin': stupid bloody blackfellas ... You fellas, you know why them *wetjalas* marchin' down the street ... I'll tell youse why. 'Cause them bastards took our country and them blackfellas dancin' for 'em.'

This is paralleled with Milly's efforts to get the kids off to school, an exchange where the younger son David, talking about the man who sells pies to the kids, announces that 'Old Tony the ding always sells us little shrivelled ones and them *wetjala* kids big *fat* ones'. The last line of the scene goes to Joe, who says, in Nyoongah, *'Allewah wilbra, gnuny barminy barkiny'.* The line is left untranslated.[6]

In a brilliantly condensed opening, Davis succeeds in establishing the central divisions which will operate throughout his play. On the one hand, we have a false celebration of white values, trumpeted by Official History in the form of a newspaper. On the other hand we have the un-official story - the silenced view making itself heard. In fact,

Joe's hesitant reading of the words in the paper reinforces how alien the message and the white language are. And by putting the two together in an uncomfortable marriage of lifestyles and ideas, Davis subtly subverts or attacks the established view of the peaceful take-over of Australia by whites, and the stereotype of the compliant native. This is our introduction to the play.

Later in *No Sugar* Davis introduces a typical Aboriginal form of theatre which precedes European forms by thousands of years - the corroboree. In Act Two, Scene Six, Billy, Joe, Jimmy and Bluey sit by a fire and paint themselves with *wilgi* in traditional fashion and then sing the various songs from their regions. To the sounds of clap-sticks, we hear Jimmy's rendition of the Crab song, which explains how to fish and where to find them. But again, this song is told in the original language, and if non-speakers want to understand, they have to turn to the appendix - to the margins. The power structure is therefore reversed.

The song suggests the disappearance of the old way of life, but it also shows how history and myth are passed on from generation to generation, in a theatrical form which is radically unlike the safe theatre of middle-class whites. Davis fuses the two. In a way which shows how oral history is self-sustaining, Jimmy's story prompts Billy to tell his own story about the Oombulgarri Massacre in which the people of the Kimberley region were slaughtered in a white ambush. The story helps to explain how Billy became a 'black crow', working against his people for the Government. We suddenly understand the pain and suffering that has forced him into his subservient and treacherous way of life.

More importantly, Billy refuses to accept Jimmy's notion that the dances - that is, the corroborees which keep their culture alive - are almost finished. Billy says, 'You song man, you fella dance men. This still your country ... [Whites] make 'em fences, windmill, make 'em road for motor car, big house, cut 'em down trees. [But it's] Still your country!' (pp. 66-67). It is a message to Jimmy, and to all Aboriginal people, to keep dancing the corroboree-to keep dancing and telling their history. It is an image which returns us to the opening of the play, where the Aborigines were dancing for the whites; telling a lie. This simple scene conveys the importance of dancing to a different tune - not to the hype and hypocrisy of the brass bands of Europe, but to the clap-sticks and didgeridoos of . Aboriginal Australia.

It would be fair to argue that what all of Jack Davis's works strive most to do is to give voice, and to stir towards action. Davis believes in the power of the story - of storytelling - whether it be in the form of dance, song, play or poetry. It is perhaps not surprising that his autobiography should end with the line, 'in presenting the triumphs and the tragedies of our lives, I hope it will inspire others to write of their lives as I have done',[7] or that his poem 'The Writers' should begin:

> *They say*
> *we are the makers of history we*
> *inspire others*
> *to laugh to cry and to kill.* [8]

'The Writers' is an uncompromising poem which recognises the double-edged sword, the power of the pen, which can uplift but also destroy, whose strokes can celebrate or vilify, this double edge is symptomatic not only of Aboriginal life, but of all life, in a society where few cultures are comfortably only one thing and not another. Jack Davis acknowledges this multiplicity of voice. He invites us to hear it for all it is worth. But in particular, he urges the voices of black Australia to speak out loudest and clearest of all.

Notes

I Oodgeroo Noonuccal and Gerry Turcotte, 'Recording the Cries of the People', *Aboriginal Culture Today*, ed. Anna Rutherford, Dangaroo Press, Sydney, NSW, 1988, p. 19.

2 Jack Davis, *Wahngin Country*, unpublished manuscript of the Black Swan Theatre Company Production, 1992. [I have preserved the spelling of *'watjella'* from the manuscript.-Ed.]

3 Jack Davis, I*n Our Town*, Currency Press, Sydney, NSW, 1992, p; 43.

4 Jack Davis, *Kullark / The Dreamers*, Currency Press, Sydney, NSW, 1982, pp. 27-28.

5 Thomas King, 'Introduction: An Anthology of Canadian Native Fiction', *Canadian Fiction Magazine*, No. 60 (1987), p. 6.

6 Jack Davis, *No Sugar*, Currency Press, Sydney, NSW, 1986. All these references are from this edition, Act One, Scene One.

7 Jack Davis, *A Boy's Life*, Magabala Books, Broome, WA, 1991, p. 142.

8 Jack Davis, *Black Life: Poems*, University of Queensland Press, St Lucia, Qld, 1992, p. 32

To My Brother Jack Davis:
A Tribute

Oodgeroo Noonuccal

Jack Davis is a poet, storyteller, playwright, politician and humanitarian.

I first met Jack in 1961 when we were in the Civil Rights movement, in an organisation called The Federal Council for the Advancement of Aborigines and Torres Strait Islanders (FCAATSI). I remember well the day he told me about a poem he had written, after we had been to a particularly frustrating and heavy conference of FCAATSI. Jack returned to Perth, Western Australia and, as was his practice, he shed his urban ways and went bush so he could sum up the conference and consider ways and means of furthering the Aboriginal and Torres Strait Islanders' Civil Rights cause.

On this particular occasion, he told me how he was sitting on a log, pondering the ways of the Western White World. He came to the conclusion that he and I were either very bad educators or that our good 'Gubbariginals' (white friends) were slow learners. It hurt him, as it did me, to see the damage done to our country - and especially to the environment - by the invaders and their descendants in the short period of two hundred years.

Jack always enjoyed communicating with his beloved Earth Mother, as is the natural way of all Aborigines. He was trying to think about what the Earth Mother would say should she wake from her sleeping place at Uluru (Ayers Rock) and witness the damage done to her beautiful creations. Jack further related that there was an unexpected, sudden rush of a strange wind which came gushing through the tall trees. He reached for his notebook and pen and wrote the words the Earth Mother sent him on her winds.

The poem was 'The First-born', and it is in my opinion his best, and I envy him. I wish it were mine. The poem begins:

Where are my first-born, said the brown land sighing;
They came out of my womb long, long ago.
They were formed of my dust-why, why are they crying
And the light of their being barely aglow.

Jack also confided to me that he believed he was the only Aboriginal man in Australia who could not throw a boomerang. In his philosophical way he finally quit trying and again put pen to paper and wrote 'The Boomerang', which ends with the lines:

Why, oh why didn't my ancestors,
Invent the bow and arrow

On another such occasion when Jack had gone bush, he saw a campfire in the distance and made his way toward it. An old Aboriginal man was sitting by the fire. When he saw Jack he invited him to share his fire and food. After a while the old man asked where he came from. Jack told him about the city of Perth and explained to him what we were trying to do in the FCAATSI movement. The old man asked many questions. Jack quickly reached for his pad and pen and another poem was born. It was called 'A Eulogy for Peace':

Why don't white man sit down quiet by fire?
Not stand up and call other country-fella liar.
What white-fella want to talk about fight for?
Everybody have plenty, still want more.

By this time Jack was spending his. waking hours obsessed with the written word. His love and compassion came clearly through all his works and most children who have read his work have told me that his poem 'My Dog', to use one example, was written especially for their dog too.
In Jack's poem 'Dingo Dingo', he brings out the sad balance of the Earth Mother's law, the 'lore' of 'Kill to Eat':

> *The dingo gorged on the flesh of the kill,*
> *Picked up the lamb in her trap-like jaws*
> *And began her run to the distant cave*
> *With the food she'd won for the hungry ones.*
>
> *A blood-red dawn had painted the east*
> *When at last she reached the edge of the range.*
> *She paused and tested the air about her,*
> *Then soft and clear she called to her young.*
>
> *In an instant,frozen, she saw the Man*
> *Between herself and the secret cave;*
> *She dropped the lamb as the bullet struck*
> *Her yellow coat ran crimson then.*
>
> *The rising sun caught the scene of death.*
> *The hunter deftly handled the kill:*
> *He thought of what he could buy his young*
> *And with a smile he turned for home.*

The poem 'Urban Aboriginal' is Jack's reply to one Minister for Aboriginal Affairs who made the statement that urban Aborigines were not true Aborigines. The poem ends with the haunting lines:

> *With Murder, with rape, you marred their skin,*
> *But you cannot whiten their mind;*
> *They will remain my children forever,*
> *The black and the beautiful kind.*

Well I remember another day, when at a FCAATSI conference Jack reported the sadness and frustration of the Laverton story. Without any show of anger, cool and calm on the outside, he related the brutality of the sorry affair. Little or nothing was done about it and the men upholding the white man's law did their best to cover the incident and play it down. This forced Jack to write about it in a poem called 'Laverton Incident'. Jack's footnote reads:

Laverton is 470 miles from Perth, WA, in the eastern goldfields area. In September 1969 an Aboriginal named Raymond Watson was wounded in the leg by a police officer during a disturbance, and subsequently died in hospital. The case caused controversy in Aboriginal circles throughout Australia.

How well Jack knew and could sum up that angry, impatient, pig-headed stubborn woman then known as Kath Walker, in his poem called 'Walker to Kath' from *Jagardoo*:

> *Fight on, Sister, fight on,*
> *Stir them with your ire.*
> *Go forward, Sister, right on,*
> *We need you by the fire.*

Jack's plays are now well known and are of deep historical, educational and cultural value. In my opinion his play *The Dreamers* is an outstanding piece of live theatre. I remember seeing this particular play in Brisbane, Queensland, at the Twelfth Night Theatre, with Jack Davis playing the role of Uncle Worru.

He is also a very fine actor. I was most concerned for his health at that time in view of the fact that he had to take a fall to the floor at every showing. He was well past his prime and the energetic performance required in *The Dreamers* must have been a very tiring time for him. However he survived all sessions, being the extremely stubborn and determined man he is.

I found it very interesting during the interval to listen to the comments of well-known theatre and television actors of non-Aboriginal descent. One actor, when asked for her opinion, was lost for words and in a confused way answered, 'Well, it's different isn't it?'. The Aborigines in the audience were rolling with laughter at the snide jokes that only Aborigines could understand.

Such is the situation when two cultures clash. It came through very clearly in The Dreamers that non-Aborigines know little or nothing about our ways, unlike the Aborigines who understand very clearly about non-Aboriginal theatre.

Jack has also taken great interest in other young writers, playwrights and poets in their creative efforts, and many of our younger writers owe him much in this respect. He is also of great value in the educational field, spending much time teaching at schools at all levels of the education system.

Many authors have written about Jack Davis's talents.

He is known all over the world for he has travelled widely to introduce audiences of all races to his plays, poems and writings. By the Aborigines he is treated with deep respect, much love and in the eyes of our young Aboriginal people, he is well known and deeply respected as an elder in his own right.

To me, he will always be a cherished brother and valued friend who will be remembered as one of the greatest artists, writers, poets and humanitarians that Australia and our Earth Mother have had the wisdom to birth.

Jack Davis, it is my pleasure to write this tribute.

Your sister Oodgeroo salutes you with much love and top honours. Your songs will be sung long after both you and I have returned to the. loving arms of our Mother Earth.

May the ink in your pen never dry up.

'The Real Australian Story':
An Interview with Jack Davis

Adam Shoemaker

[Conducted at Jack Davis's house in Fremantle, WA on the afternoon of 4 July 1992.]

AS: About ten years ago we spoke in Canberra about what might happen in black Australian literature over the next decade. You said then that you thought there would be a blossoming in the field, with Aboriginal people writing, not one or two books, but thirty or forty.

JD: Yes! It has happened, and we've got lots of writers in Western Australia and there are quite a few in the eastern states. I think we have more writers in this state than the eastern states have, and that speaks well for what is happening in Western Australia.

AS: That's an interesting thing, isn't it? Why do you think that WA has had more than its fair share - especially in drama?

JD: I think maybe because we've had a few writers who've stuck to the task. Like myself for instance - and Sally Morgan, who has come along later - and of course Mudrooroo. We've been there at the back of it all the time doing something, pushing out something. And we've helped the others along the road and now we're getting the results from it.

AS: Do you actually get together often with other writers?

JD: No. Lots of telephone meetings, but apart from that we don't get together very often.

AS: Do you see education as one of the main roles of your works: that is, plays not necessarily being performed in theatres but being read in school-rooms?

JD: Yes. All Aboriginal writing should be read in schools, and there's a big push towards getting that done today. We won't see the outcome of that for a few more years, but I think it is going to help us.

AS: Some critics (many of them poets themselves) have said that they think that you're a great playwright but a lousy poet. How do you respond to that?

JD: Well, people are allowed their own opinions. That's all I can say, Sometimes I think I'm a better playwright than I am a poet and sometimes I think I'm a better poet than I am a playwright. Out of both genres I like writing poetry the best of the two. Maybe I am a poet at heart and not a playwright.

AS: Which of the two forms do you think is closer to traditional Aboriginal oral narrative? Drama or poetry?

JD: I think drama, because drama does give you a special look at the Aboriginal, a slice of Aboriginal existence or life. And I think that's much clearer than what poetry is - what my poetry is, anyway.

AS: Now that's interesting, because when you look at your drama you have non-Aboriginal characters in plays such as Kullark and *In Our Town* as well as the central black Australian roles. Do you think you could ever write a play with totally non-Aboriginal characters?

JD: Oh yes. I don't see why not. The fact is I don't want to, because I'm writing about the things that I'm familiar with - the things which I've seen happening in my lifetime. But I could, if I wanted to, write one with all non-Aboriginal characters. I wouldn't feel constrained.

AS: It seems that *In Our Town* fits in between some of the other plays. It's set about ten years after *No Sugar* isn't it? Before *The Dreamers* and before *Barungin*?

JD: Yes. But in terms of time, I think you could really place *In Our Town* whenever you wanted. As long as it's after *No Sugar;* you could place it after *Barungin* if you wanted to. It doesn't really have to be before *Barungin*.

AS: So it's not so much the time as the attitude? Is that right?

JD: That's right, yes.

AS: One of the things I noticed is that it's the first play you have written which revolves around a love story, at least in part. Is the message of *In Our Town* that Aboriginal/white relationships can work?

JD: I think it's just people standing up for themselves. Miscegenation would come into it, I suppose, if people wanted to look at it from that point of view. But the fact of miscegenation: I wasn't even trying to solve that or point that out. I just wrote it because the romance was there - and I wanted to follow it up as just a romance between two people.

AS: And once again, the police play a big part. You still have no love for them, I take it?

JD: Well, I mean in all country towns in Australia those people are 'it'. The police are in charge. You have your country mayor or your Road Board officials - they are all minor figures - but the big boss cocky is always the police, usually the police sergeant.

AS: This links in with some of your other plays, doesn't it. *Barungin* is set in 1988 in the shadow of the Royal Commission Into Black Deaths in Custody, which was taking place at the time. Do you feel it's important for your plays to come out at particular moments when they can comment on current political and social events?

JD: I think it's necessary because we need the publicity. *Barungin* came out at the time of the 'Deaths in Custody' syndrome and *Kullark* came out when we first started to become political. *No Sugar* was a political play also. They were all written for a reason.

AS: Had you ever seen the film *Cry Freedom*? I ask because of the end of that film, when they're listing the names of all of those who've died in custody. Was there any link between that and the end of *Barungin*?

JD: Yes, because I saw *Cry Freedom* and I used the same technique. And it worked well in both cases.

AS: How do you feel about those plays which you've acted in yourself? Are you closer to those than the ones you've written but haven't acted in?

JD: Ahhh, perhaps in some special way I suppose, but I really don't think in terms of one play being a favourite over another. I don't think that has happened or matters. Because I think my favourite play is one which you haven't mentioned, and that's *Moorli and The Leprechaun.* That's a little play which I like very much.

AS: That's the only one I haven't seen. Could you tell me a bit about it?

JD: Well it's about two mythical spirits - a leprechaun and a Moorli - who meet in Australia and they decide to cure this racist guy (who lives in this town) of his racist tendencies. And they become friends with an Aboriginal boy and a white girl. And the two spirits combine to help these two - this young couple - to achieve what they want; to be able to go away on a basketball trip to Alice Springs. And there's all sorts of action between the two spirits and the girl's father ... and away they go: quite a nice little package.

AS: Is it directed at a certain age group or is it for everyone?

JD: It's for everyone--from eight to eighty.

AS: Getting back to *The Dreamers*, some observers - like Mudrooroo for example - feel that it's your best play. And the reason they say that is because they feel it has more of the spiritual and supernatural element of Aboriginal life in it, whereas a work like *No Sugar* is more realistic, naturalistic. Do you want to comment on that?

JD: I think that's right. I think there was more of a spiritualistic attitude in *The Dreamers* than there was in *No Sugar. No Sugar* was set just before World War 11 - three or four years before the war - and the characters were all in different age groups; they made up the family group. Whereas in *The Dreamers* the old man Worru was the one with the spiritual link to the past. There was no spiritual link in *No Sugar*.

AS: Did you write *The Dreamers* with yourself in mind to play the role of Worru?

JD: No. No, I never wrote it with myself in mind, but I wrote it because that character was very much like my father-in-law, when I first got married. But Worru actually comes from several characters and so, out of several old Aboriginal men, the character of Worru was born.

AS: So who suggested you should play that role then? Was it Andrew Ross?

JD: Yes. Andrew suggested I should play Worru.

AS: The reason I ask is because the role seems to fit you so well; it seems to fit your character.

JD: Well I know the character so well that I didn't have any trouble in doing it. Like I played Billy Kimberley in *No Sugar*; I know Billy Kimberley well. So I was able to play the character quite well because I knew him as a figure in Moore River when I was a boy.

AS: I noticed that your latest play - *Wahngin Country* - was not directed by Andrew Ross but by Michael Leslie.

JD: Well, Andrew did help a little with it. But he was busy working on Sally Morgan's *Sistergirl* - and they were both playing at the same time. Michael did it in conjunction with Andrew, but mainly he did it himself.

AS: Were the dynamics of the play any different with an Aboriginal director?

JD: No. No, there was no real difference. Wahngin Country was a one-man show. The guy who acted in it - Stephen Albert

- was from Broome. And of course he acted it right from the word go, using Aboriginal pathos and Aboriginal stories; it was quite funny and linked up pretty well together. So there was no real difference between that play and the others except that it was written for just one man and he was an Aborigine.

AS: Would you have dreamt ten years ago that you'd be looking back at five, six or seven successful plays at this stage?

JD: No, I wouldn't have thought that I'd have turned out that many. But from the first one I wrote I wanted to write more; I felt like writing more - so I did. My energy and my enthusiasm has fallen away a bit now, but I've put out quite a large number.

AS: It seems that you sort of caught fire between 1984 and the end of the decade. How do you feel when your plays are performed overseas? Do you feel your work has a different impact on overseas audiences than on Australian audiences?

JD: I think it has a bigger impact locally than it has overseas because local people know a lot of the story and so they're interested in seeing what happens in the play format. *No Sugar* was very well-received in Canada; there was more comment in Canada than we got in London, as a matter of fact. Because I think in London it was just another play - sort of exotic. But Canadian people: well they did ask lots of questions and there was lots of feedback from people.

AS: Jack, one of the words which is almost always associated with your drama is 'Aboriginality'. What do you think this term means? '

JD: I find it difficult to answer that because I wasn't brought up in a camp. I never had anything to do with a reserve situation until I was about fourteen, when I went to the Moore River Settlement. Before that I lived in a street something like this - in a house something like this - know what I mean? So all my reflections go back from when I was fourteen until now and I don't know: what is Aboriginality? What does it mean? It means something to Mudrooroo, something to me, something to different people in different ways. I mean if you ask the average kid today - an Aboriginal kid in the street - to go and track a horse I don't think he could track a horse through a bog! The same as any other white kid today. So you know, where is Aboriginality today? I find it difficult to try and find out what we mean by Aboriginality.

AS: Do you think it's partly an attitude?

JD: Yes. It's a state of mind. From my point of view, it's a state of mind. I mean, I would defend myself being an Aboriginal because I think that's great and I love being an Aboriginal. I'm proud of it and in one way I've got my feet in both worlds. I've got my feet in the white world and I have also got my feet in the black world. That gives me a way of looking at things which is maybe a little different from what other people do. And that's why I think the term 'Aboriginality' is a bit of a misnomer. Well, it is for me anyway.

AS: Do you think that nearly all Aboriginal people have - if not their feet - then maybe a few toes in the white world as well?

JD: That's right. They have to, to exist. I mean the urban Aboriginal - he's still got his wristwatch on, you know, to keep track of time.

AS: Do you think that what is crucial is who controls the process; whether or not black Australians control their own destiny?

JD: That's another way of looking at it but I don't think that's quite Aboriginality myself. There has to be a term between it - what we know of as being an Aboriginal way back, one hundred years ago or one hundred and twenty years ago or one hundred and fifty years ago - and what an Aboriginal is today. Because we no longer have to eat off the dirt, we no longer have to suffer the things we suffered even twenty or twenty-five years ago. Things are totally different and they're there if we need them.

AS: Am I hearing you say that you think the situation has improved for Aboriginal people in the last thirty years?

JD: That's right; yes.

AS: Some would disagree with that. I mean, some would say that with health problems, with deaths in custody, that maybe things have improved in some areas but in others they've become worse. How do you feel about that?

JD: Well that is the march of time, I suppose. Deaths in custody need not have happened, need not ever have happened if we'd got off on the right foot say twenty, twenty-five, thirty years ago. We got off on the wrong foot - or maybe we got off on the right foot and then we were pushed off onto the wrong foot. We don't really know because you would need more than me to be able to nut that one out. You would need a psychologist with a pretty big degree to be able to nut out the reasons why we have deaths in custody. Because, you know, Aboriginal youth is disrupted, and there are unfortunate people who cut off their noses to spite their own faces.

AS: But has the Royal Commission actually achieved anything!

JD: Oh, they must have achieved something. I mean, the whole situation has improved throughout Australia. Since the report there have been less deaths in custody. We know that. In fact, I don't think we've had any in Western Australia. I've only heard of them elsewhere. So it must have had some impact. Something must have been bettered, otherwise it would have continued. Whether it's these Draconian laws which have been set up; whether that's frightened youths into pulling their heads in a bit we don't know. But it's certainly improved since then.

AS: Rhoda Roberts pointed out recently on SBS that a higher number of Aboriginal women had died over the past decade from domestic violence than the number of Aboriginal men who died in custody. Does that surprise you?

JD: No, it doesn't surprise me because some Aboriginal men have been really harsh on their women, on their families. That's one of the reasons why kids are off the rails, because there's been no family life. And I believe what Rhoda Roberts has said, that more women have died than men have in the same period.

AS: What do you think the solution is - what is to be done!

JD: Well if I could answer that I'd solve a lot of problems throughout the. world, let alone in our own backyard. I don't know; we need stricter laws too, where the police can go in and arrest someone in domestic arguments, because at the present moment they're not able to. If those laws come out and if they strengthen them a bit, maybe we'll be able to cut down on the deaths and the family disputes.

AS: Do you think that there's a role in outback communities for what is called Customary Law or Tribal Law - instead of the white man's law?

JD: Ahhh. I'd be very careful with that one because I mean, practically wherever you go today, Aboriginal people are used to the white man's law. As I've said before, they're no longer used to their own law. Their own law has slipped away and we might confuse them more by wanting to go back. It might be better if we went forward. I think if we go forward with the help of Aboriginal people themselves, we'll probably be able to find things will improve.

AS: We're talking about literature but we're talking about politics a lot here too.

JD: Well if you're Aboriginal then you're a politician. If you're black, you're political.

AS: Do you feel, looking at poetry, that it can it be more political than drama?

JD: Yes, it can be political, but I don't think it can be quite as specific as drama can. But the politics are there. It's up to the poet to be able to bring that out: to be able to develop the politics of poetry, bring it out, bring it forward. I think a lot of Oodgeroo's poems are political, and I think some of mine are quite political too. So it can be the case; but I don't think they'll be quite as political as the plays can be.

AS: Mind you, you always have poetry in your plays anyway!

JD: Yeah, that's right.

AS: Of course, your work often focuses on history, whether or not the plays are set in the past. Some critics feel that you try to redefine time in your drama by having, for example, the dream sequences in *The Dreamers* at the same time that Nyoongah people are sitting around their kitchen table. Were you trying to say that the past exists in the present?

JD: Yes. I think it does because we draw the past; we bring it with us. People have often said to me, 'Oh you can forget those things; this is 1992. Just forget it - that happened in the past: But the fact is that the past is related to the present and the present is related to the future. The three of them are combined together and that happens to be existence. We cannot be unless that is so, because that is part of living.

AS: Do you think that white Australians are trying to deny the past?

JD: They're trying to deny us the Aboriginal past. They would like us to forget it and get along and try and be nicely assimilated. They say everything will be all right when we forget what's happened in the past.

AS: What do you feel is the value of your plays when they're performed live? Is this more valuable than when they're in published form?

JD: Well, personally I like to see them on stage. I like seeing the actual performance and then the whole thing breathes as it were and it's there in a three-dimensional style you can see. Reading it is not quite as good. Though of course, seeing the play and then reading it gives you quite a kick because you've seen it in three dimensions - now you see it in two dimensions - and that's good.

AS: What is it that is lost when the play is published?

JD: I think it depends upon, say, if you're in a classroom and your teacher or your tutor is reading a play to you or getting you to analyse it. It depends upon that teacher or tutor whether or not they can make the play come alive to the ones who are trying to understand it. So, I think with the proper handling it can be made quite good entertainment--quite good for students even.

AS: Have you been to classrooms which are studying your plays?

JD: Oh, yeah.

AS: How do you encourage them to do it?

JD: Well they ask the questions and it's up to me to prompt and answer their questions. They become really animated - especially those who've seen the play and they've passed on their knowledge of some of the story to the other students beforehand, and then the whole thing becomes quite good.

AS: Have they ever asked you a question you couldn't answer?

JD: Ahhh, no ... yes, one little girl did. One little ten-year-old girl, once. I was talking about - I think it was *Kullark* but I'm not too sure - and we were talking about the Dreaming tracks, and I said, 'This line here' (I had the map on the wall) - 'This line here represents the Dreaming tracks where the people went through and this one is a circumcision track'. One little girl said, 'What's the circumcision track?' and I said, 'You ask your teacher!' I had to defer on that one!

AS: Jack, one perennial problem with plays is, how do you get over the fact that most Aboriginal people can't afford to go to the theatre and see them? The ticket prices are just too high.

JD: That's right. They're higher now than they've ever been. Well, with my plays we've always managed to get Aboriginal people in. If not for nothing, as low as we possibly can. But it's one problem that is very difficult to get over unless you have special nights for Aboriginal people.

AS: Another dilemma concerns the non-Aboriginal audience. Do you think that because of the cost, you are preaching to the converted if you are presenting plays to people? That they're not going to bother to spend that much unless they are already sympathetic to what they're seeing?

JD: Yes. Well, I mean you've got that difficulty with anything if you are on a platform preaching politics. From a soapbox in the park you've always got that. And there's always someone else who is going to come along and heckle you because they are the opposition. That's one of the things that you just have to put up with.

AS: Have you ever been heckled in a performance?

JD: No.

AS: Why do you think that is?

JD: People either believe that I'm right or they're too polite or the other. I've never ever been heckled.

AS: What would you say your greatest moment as a writer has been?

JD: I don't know. There have been lots of moments. I don't think there's ever one particularly great moment. I think there have been several throughout my career as a writer. Getting a four-year Creative Fellowship grant was good-that was a great moment, and I was recognised. Getting the BHP Award was a great moment too. There are lots of things. I can't pick just one out specifically. There have been quite a few.

AS: To be fair, I should ask you the reverse too: what would you say was one of your most disappointing moments as a writer?

JD: I don't really think I can recall anything - not a disappointing moment. No; I don't think I can recall one.

AS: When you think of it, how many careers do you think you've actually had?

JD: I think one as a poet, one as a playwright. Certainly one as an educationalist. That would just about cover it.

AS: And then some people would list you as a stockman...

JD: Oh, yes.

AS: Boundary rider, fence-mender...

JD: Yeah, that's right.

AS: It seems to me that you could be like a one-man CES.* (The Commonwealth Employment Service)

JD: Right!

AS: You know, all the occupations.

JD: Right.

AS: But when I tell people overseas about you they don't believe it. They can't believe it's possible for someone to have done all those things and then suddenly change tack and become a dramatist. What enabled you to do what other people have to stud), for years to be able to do?

JD: I think it was because of black politics. I think that was one of the main reasons. And I'd had a fairly - I was pretty well bashed around the head with Shakespeare when I was at school. I finished up hating him, disliking him. It was only when I started writing plays myself that I really woke up to what William Shakespeare was about, what a great playwright he was. But I saw something on television once - I forget what the name of it was - but it dealt with play-writing and that gave me an idea. So I wrote this story which was going to be a novel, sent it to a friend and he said, 'Why not turn it into a play?'.

AS: Was that *The Biter Bit*?

JD: No, that was before that. I kept it at home for a while and then I wrote *The Biter Bit*, of course, in Sydney and came back and that gave me some ideas about this thing I'd left behind. So I rang this guy again and he said, 'Well I'll give you somebody's address to have a look at it', and it was Andrew Ross. So Andrew had a look at it and said, 'Make it into a play; it'll be quite good'. So I wrote it as a play and he helped me with it.

AS: Right - so that's how it all started?

JD: Yes.

AS: We've been talking about the past a lot and certainly that's covered very strongly in your autobiography, *A Boy's Life*. Did you have trouble remembering any of the events from your childhood?

JD: No, it was just a case of the harder I worked on it, the easier it became. Sometimes I'd find I'd been writing out excerpts of my life and others would crop up which I hadn't thought of for some considerable time. Then I would want to link up something in-between. That is where I've had to separate little instances, where I've separated them. But, in fact, I didn't have much of a job of it at all.

AS: So how quickly did you manage to write the whole thing?

JD: Oh, it took me about two years.

AS: Did the editors change much when it went up to Magabala Books?

JD: They suggested I should change some parts and were quite emphatic about me changing others. But all in all we worked pretty well together.

AS: Was there any occasion when they wanted you to change something and you didn't agree?

JD: No, no. In fact, where I wanted things I just said, 'I want it', and that was it.

AS: So you really had control over the book?

JD: Yes, that's important.

AS: Magabala is an interesting case: again, another Western Australian innovation. Do you think that because of where they are they have access to a whole different world of writing?

JD: At times they've said they feel isolated. It costs them a lot to ring up and all that type of thing, to start off communicating. But they're right amongst the language pools and the story pools from an Aboriginal viewpoint, and it is a black company, you know. I think they get quite a large amount of money each year from the government to run it. As long as it's a viable proposition it's likely to stay there.

AS: Do you think in a sense it might be taking the place of what *Identity* was doing in the 1970s? You know, having a black publishing company instead of a black magazine?

JD: Well, we talked about it, during the *Identity* days - about a black publishing company. But I would like to see them - it would be the ideal setting - if we had a magazine as well coming out of Magabala Books.

AS: Getting back to *A Boy's Life*, do you think things would be very different if you were growing up today?

JD: I don't think so. I think the lives of children are the same today, as they were in my day. You make your own fun and you get out of life what you can yourself. I think my day is the same as what kids are today - even if they're different settings.

AS: If there is humour in *A Boy's Life,* what kind of humour is it?

JD: Well it's grass-roots humour: written from the style of the boy first, as he is able to understand things and is able to write things down. He remembers it, and then we have the finished article.

AS: Do you think there is a sense of Aboriginal humour which is different from other types of humour - different from, say, European humour?

JD: I think Aboriginal people are more spontaneous with their humour. Quicker to laugh. They don't view life as being serious as non-Aboriginal people do. But I think all in all there's really not much difference. Except with the spontaneity between Aboriginal people and white people. Aboriginal people are more ready to laugh than whites are.

AS: In your plays, this is what some people can't understand. A lot of white members of the audience come out and say, 'But how can they be happy when they're living in such poverty?'. And some students say to me when they read your plays, 'I don't understand why the Aboriginal characters are laughing so much'.

JD: Yes, there is a different attitude to humour. I mean, Aboriginal people are able to survive because of laughter. Maybe if they didn't laugh so much they would change their situation, change the situation they're in. Maybe if they took life more seriously. They tend to hide their troubles behind laughter. And I know at times I think, 'Well, why laugh at that? Why not get up and do something about it?'. But I find myself laughing with them.

AS: So do you think that in some ways laughter can be a good thing and a bad thing?

JD: Yes. It can be good and it can be bad. Definitely. Aboriginal humour is far different to white humour. Aboriginal people see humour where white people could see it for a smile but not for a laugh. They don't laugh at it; they may grin at it but they don't laugh at it. But an Aboriginal - if he felt like it - he'd just hold his guts and roar with laughter.

AS: Well, we've talked about the past and we've talked about the present. Ten years ago you made a lot of predictions; what do you think the next decade holds for Aboriginal writers and for black Australians in general?

JD: As far as writers are concerned, I think the future looks good for them. I think it'll be good for stage and good for film. As for Aboriginal people - politically - I don't think we're going to get very far. It all depends what we're looking for. You could ask me, 'What do you mean? What do you want?' If I was asked that question I would say we need a far better go for Aboriginal people throughout Australia. I'm talking about those who live in urban and rural settings also. So there are lots of things that could be corrected in the next ten years.

AS: Do you think they will be corrected?

JD: I think so. I think we'll gradually get over them. I don't think they'll be corrected properly, but I think we can get over them. For Aboriginal people, there has to be an improvement in the living standards of everybody. There are lots of poor whites in this country as well as poor Aboriginal people, though Aboriginal people are numerically poorer than whites. But we have lots of poverty in Australia and a lot of it is hidden. There's a lot of unemployment. You only have to walk down the streets here in Fremantle and you can see the unemployed.

AS: If you were Prime Minister, where would you start?

JD: To be quite frank, I don't know. I just wouldn't know where to start. If you had said, 'I'm going to ask you that question tomorrow' and you came along I'd still say, 'I don't know'. Because it's a very big job. We have to look at the poverty in other countries as well as the poverty in Australia. We're not so poverty-stricken as other places are. A friend of mine just came back from the United States and he said it's absolutely chaotic in America. The incidence of poverty there is absolutely staggering.

AS: One of the things that people like Kevin Gilbert emphasise is Aboriginal health. He argued that you can't have education if people aren't well enough to go to school.

JD: That's right.

AS: So when you get right down to the basics it's food, shelter, health.

JD: Right, right. That always has been the reason; we've always said that. Health comes first. I mean we've always said that health, then education - or education and health together- and then further education and then employment; housing and employment go together.

AS: Do you think it'll take violence in Australia before there is real reform in Aboriginal affairs?

JD: I think so. While people are not violent, you can appease them by saying, 'Here's a few more bob. Here, start that little programme going.' You can appease them. But when things don't improve the violence must come, unfortunately. They must have that violence.

AS: So are you pessimistic or optimistic at the moment, looking ahead to the future?

JD: I'm pessimistic. Not very optimistic at all.

AS: What are you actually thinking of doing as your next project?

JD: I'm writing a number of short stories at the present moment.

AS: A collection, or just some individual stories?

JD: A collection, which I hope to have ready by next year. I'm also working on an Aboriginal dictionary - more or less a word-list; not, so much a dictionary. There were fourteen tribes in the south-east of Western Australia. Those fourteen tribes are gone but there's a smattering of the fourteen dialects still left. And everybody speaks that smattering now. Everybody understands certain words of it. Nyoongah. I want to get that all together and get it back to one language again, but Nyoongah is a composite language.

AS: Sally Morgan's first play *Sistergirl* premiered this year; do you feel it is similar in any way to your plays?

JD: I think *Sistergirl* is entirely different to anything I've written. Inasmuch as she had two beds on stage from the beginning to the end - and everything took place in a hospital ward. And it had very sharp witty dialogue - it went very well.

They had record houses every night; it has toured the Northern Territory and I think they're going over east in October or November.

AS: Was the humour of the play used to make the pain more bearable?

JD: I think so. The whole idea was the hospital, Aboriginal ladies in hospital, And the ward patient is an Irish woman and of course you've got the Irish humour, you've got the Aboriginal humour - they mix quite well. And the visitor is an Aboriginal woman who visits the other Aboriginal woman and she also visits the Irish woman. And the Aboriginal woman who is in hospital, she plays one against the other to get more attention herself, from the Aboriginal visitor - because she thinks she's been paying too much attention to the Irish patient. It's quite funny right through.

AS: Did you give any advice to Sally as she was writing it?

JD: No. I saw the first draft of it when it was only about half an hour long, and she asked me 'Is it long enough?', and I said 'No; you need another hour's writing'. Sally gasped when I said that, but it was entirely her own idea.

AS: And then there are Richard Walley's plays, like *Coordah and Munjong*.

JD: Yeah, Richard's work has been quite well received. I think Richard's plays have got more politics than mine have. And I think that's good. I mean we need that, we need some political satire throughout the plays and that's one thing I haven't really done. I've more or less stuck to family, because family is the basic unit, the bedrock of Aboriginal life.

AS: And then there is Eva Johnson's work. What are some of the differences you perceive in her drama, in plays such as *Tjindarella*?

JD: I've only seen one of Eva's plays and that was a one-woman show. I saw it in Melbourne and it was very good.

AS: Do you think that of all the plays you've seen - including your own - that many of them could be made into feature films?

JD: Yes, there's some good material there. I think *No Sugar* would make a good film. I think *Coordah* would make a very good film also - there's lots of material there for somebody to get up and say, 'OK, let's make a film out of it'. Oh, yes, there's good scope there.

AS: One of the reasons I ask is because you really excel at writing dialogue. Where do you get it from? Are you actually copying speech that you've heard or do you make it all up?

JD: Mostly, it comes out of my own head. But I am conscious of the way Aboriginal people speak. And when you copy the way they speak the humour comes out of that. So I don't have much difficulty in creating humorous situations. Once they create the situation then I can add the dialogue. Once my characters begin their antics then the dialogue comes from that.

AS: Another aspect which seems to be prominent in your work is a critique of Christianity. What is your perspective on this?

JD: I think I'm having a gentle dig at Christianity, because this is more of a life where the missionaries are there and they try to pressure the children and pressure the adults and try to pressure everyone they can. And I think I'm having a gentle dig at them. Not too badly but I'm having a dig at the fact that they are part of Aboriginal existence; therefore, they have to be recognised and they are recognised.

AS: Has the church done anything good for Aboriginal people?

JD: No. No. Overall, from the early days of Christianity, no good came out of it. They helped to destroy Aboriginal culture. They did not permit talking in Aboriginal languages and they separated the children from their parents.

AS: So, of all those forces that you've talked about in your plays - the forces of religion, the police and the government - which has been the most harmful for Aboriginal people?

JD: Oh, I think you would have to say the police because the police are not just carrying out government policies. So I'd have to say the police. In the early days of settlement, it was the policemen who shot Aborigines and the police are still here today. We're saying off-handedly that the police are responsible for Aboriginal people dying in prison. So we're still blaming the police whether it's 1992 to 1892 or 1850.

AS: Would having more Aboriginal people in the police be just like having more Billy Kimberleys?

JD: No, I think it's a partial solution. I think if you have Aboriginal people in the police force it helps us and creates a dialogue within the force itself. It's not just a matter of police saying, 'Oh well, I never met an Aboriginal person before I became a policeman'. He doesn't meet his first Aboriginal as a prisoner, as a lot of them do.

AS: If you were advising an Aboriginal person who came to you and said, 'I want to write a play', what would you say? What advice would you give?

JD: I'd tell them research and stickability - that's all they need. Do the research properly and have the gumption to follow it right through when it finishes; it's very difficult to write plays! And not only the dialogue. You have to keep in your mind the size of your set. You've got to keep that in mind while you're writing. There are so many things you have to keep on remembering, because some of your characters can only move in a certain direction and there is so much to do ... you feel your way as you go. I have been guilty of writing half a play then writing the rest of it separately - of writing practically the last quarter of it anyway. Then I join them together - that's one way of doing it.

AS: Do you ever surprise yourself with the direction that it takes?

JD: Oh yes. Quite often. I'm often surprised at the way it does turn out-which is often entirely different to what you thought of originally. It's quite surprising.

AS: So is there any story in Aboriginal Australia that you think is crying out to be told that hasn't yet been told?

JD: I think they've all been told. But a lot haven't been told enough - and quite a lot haven't been told properly. Everything's been said but I think there's a lot we still have to learn.

AS: Yes. I have a feeling that we've only started to discover - as you put it in your poetry - 'the real Australian story'. Thank you, Jack.

Oral Culture, Theatre, Text: Jack Davis's Plays

JOANNE TOMPKINS

Jack Davis is one of the first published Aboriginal playwrights.[1] and certainly the most well-known. His entertaining - yet confronting - plays actually bring about the redefinition of concepts such as 'Australian history' and 'Australian drama' in order fully to acknowledge the presence and contributions of Aborigines to Australia.

As Mudrooroo Narogin explains in *Writing from the Fringe*, 'drama' did not exist prior to the arrival of whites in Australia; the oral tradition that provides the basis for Aboriginal histories has, however, always consisted of song, music, dance and storytelling, elements which inevitably become central to the Aboriginal practice and experience of drama.[2] The combination of theatre conventions and the oral culture alters the dramatic experience so that Aboriginal drama must be watched and read differently from white drama. Davis explains how the oral tradition intersects with Western dramatic forms when he notes that Aborigines are inherently actors whenever they interact with the white world:

You see, we've always been acting. Aboriginal people are the greatest actors in the world ... We've acted up before magistrates, we've acted up before the police, we've acted up before social workers; we've always done our own Mime.[3]

Davis has written six plays, as well as two children's plays, *Honey Spot* (1985) and *Moorli and the Leprechaun* (1994). *Kullark* was the first, written to protest the commissioning of Dorothy Hewett's *The Man from Mukinupin* for Western

Australia's Bicentennial in 1979. *Kullark* is on one level the Yorlah family living in Western Australia in 1979; it is also the story of the Nyoongahs' (the term for Western Australian Aborigines) reactions to the arrival of the first whites, who established the Swan River Colony in 1827. The play becomes a history lesson of the largely ignored Aboriginal past. The play's backdrop cleverly juxtaposes the different versions of history: the Western explorers' map of the Swan River bisects the painting of the Nyoongah creative agent, the Rainbow Serpent.

The Dreamers (1982) chronicles the history. of the urban Wallitch family. There are also frequent appearances of an increasingly degraded and oppressed Nyoongah family in the background. The other figure who dances in and out of the play's main actor is the Dreamer, seen only by the elderly Worm and his great-nephew, Shane. Shane learns through Worm and the Dreamer how to maintain contact with the Aboriginal heritage that he is in danger of losing.

First performed, in 1985, *No Sugar* explores the missions on which Aborigines were forced to live for almost fifty years of this century, although the play's specific focus is the 1930s. The play details the hardships that the mission inhabitants endured, including forced moves from places where families had lived for generations, squalid living conditions at the missions, severe food rations, inhumane punishments, and sexual abuse. Despite these circumstances, the Millimurras survive, and it is this will to survive that concludes the play.

Barungin (premiered in 1988) deals with Aboriginal deaths in custody. The most horrifying of the plays, *Barungin* correlates the black deaths and everyday lived experiences of Nyoongahs with their historical treatment. Nevertheless, this play demonstrates the vibrancy, persistence and resistance of the Aboriginal heritages, and how they continue to survive, even if in hybridised forms.

One of Davis's most recent plays, *In Our Town*, was performed in 1990, and published in 1992. It concerns the post-World War II experiences of returning Aboriginal servicemen who fought alongside whites, but who must return to the Australian society's racism after the war.

The active functioning presence of the oral culture is the most significant aspect of Davis's work, and the focus of this chapter. Oral culture, the means for communicating history and religious systems, and for entertaining, distinguishes Aboriginal drama from white drama. Davis incorporates the oral cultural devices of storytelling, song, dance, music and history in his multilingual play form to insist that Aborigines and their cultural experiences be more prominently and positively recognised and acknowledged.

Davis's characters frequently tell stories such as Worru's explanation in *The Dreamers* of the transmigration of souls, and what happens to initiated men once they die. The stories (usually in a combination of English and Nyoongah languages) explain the world in a different way than does 'scientific reasoning'. Not just a means of entertainment, the stories are also a form of education. Granny Doll relates the meaning of the family's name in *Barungin* when she explains that the surname; Wallitch, is an anglicised version of *wallitj*, the Nyoongah word for night hawk. Black audience members can recall their own family origins, while white audience members learn another way of reading genealogy. Such stories describe, for instance, which animals can be killed for food and which cannot. They suggest the importance of the land in explaining both the source of food and family songlines. The stories, then, entertain and teach both whites and blacks, but what they teach blacks is different from what they teach whites: blacks learn about their land, its origins, and their relationship to that land; whites learn about the vast knowledge that Aborigines have about this continent, and that there are many non-white ways of knowing and understanding the land.

A second way in which Aboriginal frames of reference are foregrounded over the more widely recognised white ways is in the use of 'other' languages. Nyoongah words throughout the plays become important political *and* dramatic devices. The words make very clear that English is not the only language in Australia. In the dramatic sense, the glossary at the end of the plays (and sometimes the bracketed explanations within the text) helps the reader and the actor, but the theatre audience does not have access to these translations. For the audience, the action on stage is generally enough to communicate the sense of the Nyoongah words. As a result, the language becomes accessible to people who have never before heard Nyoongah words. Occasionally there are passages in Davis's plays that are not translated, and would be difficult to understand in performance. Gran's mourning song at the end of *No Sugar* communicates grief, but the exact words of the song would be incomprehensible to non-Nyoongah speakers. This distancing device does, however, demonstrate to whites the enormous impact of being forced to learn and speak a vastly different language. Some things cannot be translated; some knowledge is truly different.

The Nyoongah words also give credibility to the country's original inhabitants. They are granted the independence that language signifies: too often the explorers who arrived in Australia did not credit the Aborigines with the cultural autonomy that a distinct language group suggests. At the beginning of *Kullark*, when black meets white for the first time, the dialogue, carried out in two different languages, expresses in both languages the fear and curiosity that everyone feels. Once the surprise of contact with the whites is over, Yagan and his fellows in *Kullark* communicate quite readily in a pidgin form of English, but virtually all the English people refuse to learn the Nyoongah language. As

Yagan and the others are killed or Christianised, the frequency of Nyoongah decreases so that in *The Dreamers*, Shane only knows one word of Nyoongah, and that is *wetjala*, ironically the word for 'white'. In *Barungin*, Granny Doll expresses the enormity of the loss of language: '*Wetjalas* killed our language.'[4] This death is specific and metaphoric: without a language, the people die too.

Davis's plays reflect the wide variety of Aboriginal musical interests: Peter's taste for disco in *The Dreamers* contrasts with the Yorlahs' preference for country music in *Kullark*, while in *Barungin*, Peegun and Shane combine didgeridoo and guitar in a traditional/folk style. In other words, Aborigines are not identified by just didgeridoos. Peegun, busking in Fremantle, explains to his audience that the didgeridoo is thousands of years old, much older than the guitar. After relating how the didgeridoo is made, he and Shane sing 'The Magpie Song'. It begins like many Nyoongah songs, telling the story of a bird or animal. It shifts, though, to become a pointed cry for land rights:

> *You believe in land rights too.*
> *You believe in land rights too.*
> *Do you believe in land rights too?* (p. 16)

Just as the busking act includes didgeridoo and guitar, the song connects the traditional repeated 'songlines' with current Nyoongah concerns. The combination demon-strates the ways in which Nyoongah lives have changed as a result of white colonisation, but that change is not just a shift to white ways of life; the Nyoongah traditions are still foregrounded.

Other songs in Davis's plays include the ironic use of English hymns, such as 'There is a happy land', which appears in several of Davis's works. The English version is a hymn of praise to Jesus, but in *No Sugar*, the Aborigines parody the song, much to A. O. Neville's distress:

> *There is a happy land,*
> *Far, far away.*
> *No sugar in our tea,*
> *Bread and butter we never see.*
> *That's why we're gradually*
> *Fading away.*[5]

This song in particular expresses the Nyoongahs' displeasure with the overwhelming presence and power of the whites: the happy land that they used to live on has been taken away from them, and their happiness continues to fade as the white 'Protector of the Aborigines' cuts food rations for the mission Nyoongahs even further.

Dance is also important in Davis's plays, and the staging presence that dance brings to drama represents another way that Aboriginal customs replace white forms, particularly in *The Dreamers*. Act One, Scene Four ends with Peter dancing drunkenly to disco music from the radio. Worru, laughing at Peter's version, demonstrates what 'real' dancing is. Worru's partly remembered tribal dance recalls his youth. The play shifts when Worru's drunken legs fail to support him, and the Dreamer figure takes over the dance: *'against a dramatic red sky, [he] dances down and across in front of them, pounding his feet into the stage'*[6] What began as a nostalgic glance becomes a highly expressive - indeed militant - act as the Dreamer's dance communicates his outrage at being excluded from the white world. This action provides more than mere entertainment: through dancing, Worru 'becomes' the Dreamer, the initiated man who is, in the time of the play, a rarity. The dance also centralises the black body, focusing audience attention positively on a powerful figure who communicates the past and the present in a 'language' other than words.

The corroboree, a more formal dance and an expression of Aboriginal community and independence, communicates and reinforces traditional values in *No Sugar*. Sam, Joe, Jimmy and even the two trackers, Billy and Bluey,[7] prepare for a corroboree at the mission. The government forces them to live in virtual squalor, but they still sing a praise song that tells of abundant food, in ironic contrast to the meagre rations they are given at the mission. Even though the Millimurras and Billy and Bluey are members of different 'countries', and Billy and Bluey are otherwise vilified as trackers, all the men find a point of intersection talking about the meanings of songs or body paintings. It is the remembering of those days that gives the family the strength to endure despite the cruel treatment of the whites. The loud, moving, exciting corroboree contrasts with the dour, sober, passive, dance-less celebration of the *wetjalas*, whose Australia Day ceremony in *No Sugar* inspires no one.

Song, dance and the Nyoongah language help to express the Aboriginal views of history and time. Concepts of history are central to Davis's plays, though history here means much more than Australia Day represents. Aboriginal history 'begins' well before the arrival of the First Fleet, but since Aboriginal experiences of the past are generally not recorded in history books, Davis makes use of other texts which detail and communicate the past, including diaries, oral stories, journals, letters, transcripts of meetings, and lectures. As well as existing in other types of texts, the Aboriginal past is not confined to history: it exists within the present and the future in Aboriginal cultures. While European written language and history operate in a linear chronology, the Aboriginal understanding of the past is less fixed. For example, if an ancestor's spirit lives in the *moodgah* tree, as Worru explains in *The Dreamers*, then the dead ancestor still lives within the living tree. While the plays' contemporary storylines frequently advance in a somewhat chronological (Western) time frame, there are often characters in Davis's plays who depict the Aboriginal concept of time and history in a much more overt manner. *The Dreamers* and *Kullark* include a figure who represents pre-contact (not prehistoric) Aboriginality and who defies Western concepts of 'reality' and chronology. These characters are closely connected to the oral tradition.

The use of various forms to communicate 'history' is particularly important in *Kullark*. Several versions of the slaughter of Yagan and his tribal family are relayed, such as Yagan's own songs and Alice's diary, but only Stirling's version is accepted as the 'true' voice of history. The white documentary form, however, is turned back on itself with the addition of the black perspective in the play. When Stirling suddenly, without foundation; constructs the blacks as evil, the alternative forms of recording the past - diary, journal, debate and oral culture - illustrate that the official white version of history itself is full of lies and manipulations in the name of power. Inaccuracies are overlooked in the fabrication of white history. *Kullark* removes the power from white history to ensure that other peoples' voices are also heard.

While Davis's plays attempt to express the validity of Aboriginal history and forms, they also recognise that it is impossible to restore the pre-contact world. Aborigines must inevitably live in the white world, even if they maintain their own heritage and modify that white world. The larger Australian world cannot be ignored. The plays acknowledge this by hybridising many experiences. Numerous Aboriginal traditions are combined with white ones, such as Peegun's combination of didgeridoo and guitar in his busking routine. Hybridising does not mean assimilating: there is no suggestion that the 'Aboriginal' will be lost in an enhanced, enriched or expanded 'white' culture.

Hybridity is possible in form and content. The speeches that are highlighted in *Barungin* mix a non-theatrical form with theatre. Robert's speech to the Rotary Club in *Barungin*, then, hybridises form and content as he retells. Australian history from the Aboriginal perspective. He not only changes what is told as history, but how it is told. Robert re-presents (for whites) contact history in an oral culture form. Punctuated by Western historical reference points, Robert's speech highlights yet another example of the oral traditions in a world that prefers to recognise the written text.

The plays, mindful of both positive traditions and devastating nightmares of the past, endeavour to establish a phase of history which is in the process of being written: the future, when both the Aboriginal past and white history are celebrated. By adding Aboriginal senses of the past to the Western theatre model, the plays remain distinct from Western drama. *In Our Town* concludes with the Millimurras determined to inhabit the predominantly white town, symbolising the existence of possibilities for white and black histories, not simply 'alongside' each other, but learning how to 'come to terms' or to negotiate with each other.

Davis's plays are remarkably celebratory, despite the terrible legacy of white history that they depict. While massacres, beatings, deprivations and evictions are communicated very clearly and movingly, the plays do not just maintain that rage; they also celebrate the aspects of Aboriginal life that remain. They praise the songs and dance and language and customs and humour that can forge new understandings for other Aborigines and for whites.

For Davis, Aboriginal political activity is being usefully (but not exclusively) channelled into literary form. To him, Aboriginal writers are 'the most important thing we've got ... you could put up a tent today and people would laugh at it ... now, it's time for the people with the pen to take over'.[8]

As a result of 'the pen taking over', Davis's plays generate significant emotional impact when they are staged. They are both moving and disturbing, and the entire process of seeing the plays entails looking at theatre differently, just as it entails looking at history differently. *The First-born Trilogy* (consisting of *The Dreamers, No Sugar* and *Barungin*) was presented in 1988. The director attempted to stage the trilogy in alternative spaces, such as the Fitzroy Town Hall in Melbourne, rather than in a 'conventional' theatre. To accentuate this, the production constantly shifted to different parts of the auditorium, even requiring the audience to move to different rooms and venues within the main building. This movement captured the enforced homelessness and landlessness that whites inflicted on Aborigines. At other points, the action took place above and behind the spectators, suggesting the all-embracing nature of Aboriginal drama. The constant movement ensured that the audience did not consider the evening's events to be just like every other play they had attended.

The inclusion of elements that are essential features of Aboriginal heritage and culture, therefore, establishes Aboriginal drama as a form clearly distinct from Western drama. Aboriginal plays tend to be more of a multimedia performance, incorporating a rich pre-contactcultural tradition with current Aboriginal concerns.

Davis's plays do not merely idolise Aborigines at the expense of whites: they demonstrate the necessity of foregrounding the Aboriginal past, but they also recognise that that past is caught in the more widely accepted presence of white history. The plays, then, alter the nature of Australian history. In doing so, they also redefine Australian drama. Jack Davis's plays incorporate the oral cultural elements of Aboriginal drama into a distinctive, confronting, and highly entertaining theatrical form.

Notes

1 The first play by an Aboriginal writer was Kevin Gilbert's *The Cherry Pickers*, written in 1968, performed in 1971, but not published (in a revised form) until 1988. The first published Aboriginal play was Robert Merritt's *The Cake Man* (1978).

2 Mudrooroo Narogin, 'White Forms, Aboriginal Content', *Aboriginal Writing Today*, ed. Jack Davis and Bob Hodge, Australian Institute of Aboriginal Studies, Canberra, ACT, 1985, pp. 21-34.

3 Adam Shoemaker, *Black Words, White Page: Aboriginal Literature 1929-1988*, University of Queensland Press, St Lucia, Qld, 1989, p. 235.

4 Jack Davis, *Barungi, (Smell the Wind)*, Currency Press, Sydney, NSW, 1989, p. 36. Subsequent references will be cited parenthetically in the text.

5 Jack Davis, *No Sugar*, Currency Press, Sydney, NSW, 1986, p.98.

6 Jack Davis, *Kullark The Dreamers*, Currency Press, Sydney, NSW, 1984, p. 86.

7 Billy and Bluey are employed by the government to chase after escapees from the mission. Their participation in the corroboree indicates their preference for maintaining their traditional lifestyles: their current employment becomes just a necessary means of support to ensure survival. They are neither invited into the white world nor comfortable there.

8 Shoemaker, p. 235.

'Talking Country' : Jack Davis's Theatre

HELEN GILBERT

At a time when the Mabo debate has foregrounded Aboriginal land rights as the most crucial unresolved issue in national politics, it seems appropriate to reassess Jack Davis's theatre through a focus on its treatment of the relationships between place, history and Aboriginality. Historians such as Paul Carter have argued that the colonisation of Australia was, above all, a spatial process.[1] Linguistic, economic and cultural domination by Europeans depended on their conquest of the land as a place from which to articulate power over its original inhabitants. All of Davis's plays depict, in some way, the historical *dis*placement of Aborigines and their associated loss of identity as a consequence of over two hundred years of colonisation. But while his work details the catastrophic effects for indigenous peoples of the European *landnama* - the land-taking and land-naming - of Australia, Davis also proposes ways of reconceptualising place and space so that the legitimacy of white settlement is undermined. This paper examines the thematic and theatrical means by which his drama exposes the biases of imperialism to enact a symbolic reclamation of space/place by and for Aboriginal culture.[2]

In performance genres, unlike in fiction, narratives unfold in space as well as through time. Whereas words on a page are usually interpreted sequentially, drama offers the possibility of a simultaneous. reading, through the senses, of all the visual and aural signifiers embedded in the text as performance. Theatre thus lends itself particularly well to the representation and interrogation of the spatial aspects of imperialism. It allows a remapping of space and a reframing of time to facilitate the telling or showing of oppositional versions of the past that propose not only different constitutive events but different ways of constructing history itself. Davis exploits the flexibility of stage space/time most fully in a play such as *Kullark*, which is structured according to the principles of cinematic montage. Here, disparate images or brief scenarios are presented in sequences that defy linear chronology. The past is juxtaposed to the present and the settings are frequently overlaid so that there is no clear delineation between the spaces claimed by whites during the invasion process and the spaces occupied by blacks in the contemporary narrative. This is a deliberate technique on Davis's part and one which balances the decimation of Aboriginal culture in the historical narrative with a focus on its survival 10 the contemporary moment.

The predominantly naturalistic narratives of *The Dreamers* and *Barungin* also unfold through dramatic structures which modify linear notions of time and space. In *The Dreamers*, poetry recitals evoke the past as a ore-occurring dream' which frames the present while intermittent dream sequences fuse present, past and mythic time through spatial links between Worru, his dead friend Milbart, and the Dancer. Although we never see Milbart, his imaginary form is given presence by the Dancer and during these dreaming moments the stage is transformed into a flexible space which positions Worru in close proximity to both figures. That Worru communicates with characters from other times and places suggests the centrality to Aboriginal culture of a Dreamtime realm which co-exists with contemporary experience and continually informs it. This realm is intimately linked to the land as Davis shows through the Dancer's actions and through the framing of the lounge room setting with a backdrop featuring an escarpment on which a tribal family periodically appears.

The Dancer also appears briefly in *Barungin* to signal Peter's death and to contextualise it within a broader history of Aboriginal experience since colonisation. The funerals which begin and end this play also stress the circular movement of history, though the second funeral service is in many ways a critique of the first and a demonstration of Aboriginal solidarity against white dominance. It commemorates not only the dead explicitly named here by Meena, but also those other 'absent friends' who seem to haunt the theatrical spaces of all Davis's plays: the babies buried in unmarked graves at Moore River, the thousands of Aborigines annihilated during the initial white invasion of Australia, and those who have died since in custody.

Even when he does not construct his narratives in ways which dismantle the conventional Western conceptions of time and space, Davis frequently uses the stage to demonstrate how relationships between Aboriginal and non-Aboriginal Australians are negotiated through spatial structures. *No Sugar* and *In Our Town* are primarily plays about the contestation of the land and both explore this issue in dramatic terms through particular semiotic networks related to the setting and other aspects of the mise en scene. Using the stage space to represent enclosures, boundaries and contested places, Davis shows not only how apartheid structures are built and maintained in the interests of imperialism but also how they may be subverted or broken down. In his most recent play, *Wahngin Country*, Davis's contemporary Aboriginal protagonist continues the search for an empowering space from. which to speak as he performs, promenade-style, moving from a traditional campsite to an urban park bench while the audience follows. The title of the play, which translates as 'Talking Country', along with its particular form, asserts, once again, the links between the land and the articulation of Aboriginal identities.

That the play's initial production was staged on the grounds of the University of Western Australia suggests an attempt to counter the authority of book-learning with a celebration of orality. The performance also stressed that Aboriginal (hi)stories are often a forgotten part of the everyday spaces in which we live and study.[3] It is the function of theatre, Davis's work suggests, to make these places speak.

From the beginning of his career as a playwright, Davis has been concerned to show how indigenous spaces have been invaded and how Aborigines have been confined spatially under white colonisation. The moment of contact in *Kullark* is depicted as a territorial dispute so that when Moyarahn marks the ground with her *wahna* (digging stick) she is not simply casting a death wish on Fraser and Stirling but also inscribing her priority over the land. The backdrop, which shows the Aboriginal Rainbow Serpent repeatedly cut by revolving screens depicting on their flip sides maps and other signs of imperial presence, also indicates that the contestation of space is a crucial component of settlement. The motif of the map is important here, for as J. B. Harley has suggested, maps are a form of spatial knowledge that represents a plan, or at least a desire, to occupy and own particular territories.[4] Maps are generally assumed to convey unbiased scientific knowledge when in fact they help to maintain and justify the colonisers' control over alien space by marking out boundaries and then making them seem natural and necessary. The map of the Swan River Colony in *Kullark* shows the extent of the settlers' intended invasion and indicates the ways in which they conceptualise the land as unoccupied and merely waiting for cultivation by Europeans. By including this map as part of his backdrop, Davis demonstrates how cartography functions as an aid to colonisation; however, the play also disrupts the power of such sign systems because the map is never left intact for long and the Rainbow Serpent remains the dominant image of the set.

Although *Kullark* details the subjugation of the Aborigines and their loss of the land in the face of European military power, the authority of the colonisers is never complete or uncontested. Again, Davis's representation of the first contact is revealing for it shows the invaders at a distinct, albeit temporary, disadvantage. During one of their reconnaissance surveys, Stirling and Fraser run into a group of 'natives' but seem vulnerable and even laughable without their military support. Because they cannot control the situation, they emerge somewhat shaken from their encounter with the blacks. Their offer of clothing to Yagan and Mitjitjiroo, undoubtably meant as a 'civilising' gesture, becomes a farce when the Aborigines run off with Fraser's uniform leaving him looking decidedly ridiculous in his underwear. Further subversions of colonial rule are enacted through numerous events including Yagan's sheep stealing which, though seemingly minor, raises important ideological issues and points to the differences between settler and Aboriginal approaches to the landscape. When Yagan defends his actions by arguing that if the native wildlife belongs to everyone so too should all the produce of the land, including the sheep, he underscores the inconsistency, even hypocrisy, of white notions of ownership. Sheep 'stealing' as a small but significant act of defiance also features in *No Sugar* and *In Our Town*. In these later plays, the sheep come to represent the larger landscape which has been claimed as the property of the settlers. By their theft of the sheep, Aboriginal trickster figures such as Jimmy Munday and Uncle Herbie outwit their adversaries to achieve not only a comic victory over miserliness but also a symbolic reclamation of the land. As Uncle Herbie of *In Our Town* points out, the issue of land ownership remains debatable: 'It might be his land', he says of the white grazier, 'but it's still my country' (p. 16).

On one level it could be argued that Davis's plays illustrate the success of the imperial venture to appropriate Aboriginal land and confine its occupants to the marginalised spaces assigned to them by the dominant society. But although his theatre depicts with great clarity the containment of indigenous peoples within institutions - notably missions and gaols - designed to segregate them from white society, Davis stresses the idea of survival and resistance. Hence, what we see on stage is a representation of the world in which Aborigines are always the centre of focus, even while Davis's versions of history feature displacement and dislocation as the defining elements of black experience. Boundaries designed to delineate separate. worlds for black and white Australians frequently dissolve and become instead debatable places that speak through their violation.

A prime example of this occurs in *No Sugar* where the Aborigines repeatedly break out of the mission and refuse to respect the apartheid structures created by representatives of white authority. Although Mr Neville and Sergeant Carrol discuss the planned 'relocation' of the Northam Aborigines in terms which objectify them as part of another environmental management programme - a pest to be removed from white space - the Aborigines themselves insist on asserting their subjectivity. To disrupt their adversaries' plans, Jimmy, Milly and Gran appear on stage as speaking, moving subjects who will not be so easily eradicated. They not only interject throughout the overseers' conversation with demands to be heard, but also forcefully enter what has been inscribed as white territory, so that Neville's and Carrol's offices appear as spaces under siege. Here, Davis's use of verbal and visual counterpoint undermines the coherence, the logic, and the authority of white discourses and creates a potent image of contestation rather than segregation.

The idea of contested space is central to *No Sugar* as a whole and, ironically, it is precisely the whites' continued efforts to construct apartheid structures that emphasise the blacks' insistent visibility. Jimmy, for example, flaunts his non-compliance with the rules of the spaces assigned to him by disrupting proceedings when put in gaol. Through his amusing antics as performer and entertainer, he transforms the prison cell and the courtroom into a form of theatre where he asserts control over the spaces designed to segregate and punish him. Such subversions of 'white man's law' are widespread in Davis's plays and function to question the validity of that law. Recurrent images of imprisonment and containment are frequently framed by an Aboriginal perspective which sees incarceration as a substitute initiation for black men and therefore as part of a ritual passage into adulthood. As the events of *Barungin* remind us, however, the 'concrete floor' and the 'cell door' are also powerful symbols of oppression for Aborigines, and imprisonment remains part of the institutional brutality of colonialism which has effected the deracination of indigenous peoples and their alienation from the land.

Similarly, the removal of Aborigines from traditional homelands and their confinement on missions is shown in several plays as another form of territorial invasion which dispossesses the blacks of their land. *No Sugar* and *Kullark* detail the effects of this dislocation quite graphically and also examine its potential to effect a loss of Aboriginal identity. The missions masquerade as places constructed for the welfare of indigenes, but Davis demonstrates that such places are designed to undermine tribal and familial solidarity and to achieve the eventual destruction of the Aboriginal race. In *In Our Town*, Uncle Herbie's remarks sum up the results of the missionary drive quite succinctly: 'wetjala cunning fella alright. When they come here they had the Bible and we had the land ... Now they've got the land and we've got the Bible' (p. 44).

Equally disempowering but less openly detrimental to indigenous people is the institutionalised medical care which is linked to the mission system. No Sugar shows how medical discourses are (mis)used to justify moving the Aborigines to the Moore River Settlement to quarantine them for a disease they do not have, while The Dreamers suggests that the coloniser's medicine is largely ineffectual against Aboriginal ill health anyway. In fact, Worm seems marked for death' from the moment he first enters the corridors of the white hospital, an institution that is presented as an anathema to the survival and well-being of Aboriginal culture.

Davis's concern with the segregation and marginalisation of blacks in Australian society is reiterated from a different angle in the staged version of *In Our Town*. This play is very much about crossing boundaries and about dismantling the physical and ideological structures which disempower Aborigines and position them always at the margins of the dominant culture. For the play's premiere production in Perth,[5] these themes were stressed by a setting which. featured a diagonal line/path running from the back of the acting area to the limits of the thrust stage to mark a boundary between the predominantly white cafe-bar area and the black bush camp which occupied the rest of the set. Apart from bringing into focus the segregation of the town and, on a broader symbolic level, of the country as a whole, this setting and the actors' particular use of it fore grounded the boundary itself as a site of meaning. While some interchanges between blacks and whites were enacted with the boundary line firmly between the antagonists as a glaring barrier to communication,[6] characters like the Aboriginal youth, David, and his *wetjala* (girl)friend, Sue, were quickly established as people who transgressed such barriers, rendering them ineffective. David's frequent presence in the bar and the cafe affirmed his right to occupy white spaces while Sue made an explicit gesture of crossing over into black space to visit the Aborigines' camp. At one point, the two also walked precariously along the boundary line, a movement which symbolised their attempts to negotiate the complex spatial structures of their town/society. By framing its love story in this way, the play showed one possible path for future reconciliation between the two cultures.

The children's play, *Honey Spot*, also explores the possibility of reconciliation through an exchange of experience and cultural capital. By teaching each other their respective dances and learning to compromise, Peggy and Tim eventually put together a series of movements which utilise both the grace of the European ballet form and the vitality of the Aboriginal corroboree. The performance of this hybrid dance reinscribes the stage, and by implication, the land as shared space rather than merely the precinct of the white majority. Enactments of some kind of Aboriginal dance occur regularly in other Davis plays and are frequently used to reclaim, metaphorically if not actually, Aboriginal space/land. Because dance brings the relationship between the performing body and the territory it marks into acute visibility, it can operate as a form of protest and even a bid for land rights. The 1990 production of *No Sugar* in Perth[7] demonstrated this with dramatic flair by staging a vibrant corroboree immediately before Neville's speech to the historical society. When the dance ended, Neville walked tentatively across the corroboree ground while traces of the dancers' footsteps and a visible layer of unsettled red dust marked his presence as incongruous, invasive and ultimately illegitimate.

In *The Dreamers*, the dance functions likewise as an act of retrieval. When the Dancer appears to complete the movements which the Aborigines have long forgotten, his pounding feet remap and reclaim stage space, recuperating, for Worru and the others, the tribal dance from a position of marginality within an urban culture. *Barungin* extends this motif with the appearance, just before the funeral scene, of a dancer who links the grave-side gathering temporally and spatially to the Dreamtime and the past constructed in earlier plays of the trilogy. This dancer's presence recalls images and memories of Worru's Dreaming and of the last corroboree at Moore River. In a sense, the dancer maps out a stage space which the mourners can then inhabit, a space which resists appropriation by white figures such as the fundamentalist preacher of the opening funeral scene. The mourners then move into this space, claiming it politically, symbolically, and historically for Aboriginal people. Their wreaths of red and yellow flowers tied with black ribbons stand as metaphors for the Aboriginal flag and are therefore potent signifiers of black solidarity and nationhood. The feeling of protest this scene engenders was strengthened in the Melbourne production of Davis's trilogy in 1988 as the Fitzroy Town Hall, the chosen venue, became a site of symbolic reclamation of Aboriginal land when truckloads of sand were poured over large parts of the interior to create a suitable 'counter-bicentennial' set.[8]

In his ability to represent Aboriginal people as subjects of their own narratives rather than objects to be moved about the theatre of white history with the ease of stage props, Davis challenges the pioneer myth which ignores the possibility that Aborigines and whites moved in the same landscape. His drama suggests a spatial dimension where the two cultures interacted, where territory was contested, where Aborigines were displaced and disenfranchised. In his drama, we see the myths of colonialism rewritten, or rather replayed, as an uneasy dialogue between invader and invaded. As Australia moves towards becoming a republic in the new century, we can only hope that this dialogue achieves the reconciliation and restitution that Davis's theatre so potently urges.

Notes

1 Paul Carter, *The Road to Botany Bay: An Essay in Spatial History*, Faber and Faber, London, 1987.

2 Many of the ideas in this paper are derived from my previous work on Jack Davis's theatre. See articles listed in the bibliography for further details.

3 I am grateful to Jacqueline Lo who provided me with details of the performance of *Wahngin Country*. Directed by Michael Leslie, Black Swan Theatre Company, Perth, WA, 21 February 1992.

4 J. B. Harley, 'Maps, Knowledge and Power', *The Iconography of Landscape*, ed. D. Cosgrove and S. Daniels, Cambridge University Press, Cambridge, 1988, pp. 277-312.

5 Performed under the title *Our Town*. Directed by Phil Thomson, Marli Biyol Company, Perth, WA, 22 October 1990.

6 See, for example, the photograph in the published text which shows Mrs Moss and Milly positioned on either side of the borderline as they discuss their children's relationship. Jack Davis, *In Our Town*, Currency Press, Sydney, NSW, 1992, p. 49.

7 Directed by Neil Armfield and Lynette Narkle, Western Australian Theatre Company, Perth, WA, 1 September 1990.

8 Directed by Andrew Ross, Western Australian Theatre Company, Melbourne, Vic, 8 May 1988.

'Breaking the Rules of Theatre': Discovering Aboriginality Through Performance

ERNIE DINGO

I had heard a story that Jack Davis always carried one book, a dictionary, which he had read a thousand times. He slept with it under his pillow, so the story goes, and read it a thousand more times.

Maybe that was his way of understanding the *wetjala* who had tormented his childhood, from Yarloop where he was born to the many moves that led him to Moore River Aboriginal Settlement. Maybe that was his way of waiting for an opportunity to repay them in their own words. I don't know. But when he did put pencil to paper (or to any piece of cardboard he could find for that matter), some of the hurt he had experienced seemed to reach his tormentors and challenge their lack of understanding.

Jack Davis is a proud Nyoongah from the south-West of Western Australia. His writing was his 'release' and made him even prouder. He knew there were real stories to tell, crooked lies to be straightened - and there was the humour that had helped to maintain his dignity when the Native Welfare had control of his destiny.

In 1979 I was given my first ever acting role in his first stage production *Kullark* (or *Ghul-lar* as it should be pronounced). I walked in blind. I was good at that. My best friend, Richard Walley suggested to the director, Andrew Ross that I might be suitable. That was my introduction to theatre. No training. Didn't need any, I thought. What they were after was a young Aboriginal man and, well, I covered that area quite well. Literary, well, I could fake that.

Little did I know what lay before me.

Firstly I was late for rehearsals, then given a script and told to sit down and read it. I watched them rehearse and then it was my turn to read. Bang. That was when it hit me. It was like blasting into the world of the unknown. Not just the unknown world of theatre but the world as Jack Davis understood it.

And I had an important role to play - I was to be Jack's voice. In my solos 'Aboriginal Australia', 'Urban Aboriginal' and 'Gargoobarbut Wurrgul' I had the opportunity to portray his spirituality. I dared not mess it up.

These poems changed my attitude about myself, and every time I delivered them, I felt stronger about my Aboriginality. Singing the songs, I was becoming more confident about who I was, and, unknown to Jack, I was allowing him to shape me. He shaped my future and who I became.

During the rehearsals he was there, watching and listening like an overseer. He was a big man, peering from under his bush hat. He commanded respect and got it, I might add. As is our Aboriginal custom we called him 'Uncle Jack', and sometimes 'J. D.' and 'Drake'.

I had to learn all those words. There were pages and pages of them. I was glad when he requested that two of the poems be sung. If singing was acting, then I was already in front, because I'd sung a few songs as a 'youngfulla'. And the music added another dimension to the poetry.

My next problem was writing the music. I have always played only three chords in my life and they are the initials of my name, E, A and D. Still being my initials, they are still the only three chords that I play. They laughed about it, but to me it was like the way Jack worked, when you think about it. It doesn't take much to get the job done. If you have something to offer, even just a little bit, share it.

After *Kullark* I went to teach in Victoria. Jack, back

home in Perth, had so much more to say. He started on Production Number Two, and after a successful opening season in Perth, *The Dreamers* was destined for a national tour. I was. again invited.

The old man in *The Dreamers* was a pivotal role, and to my surprise when I turned up for rehearsals (early this time!) Jack was not only the writer but a performer. I suppose he just couldn't help himself, or as he would say, 'Someone has to do it right'. This pressured us to work even harder, not because he was also acting but because he would be watching us from on-stage.

Jack wanted to present a production cast entirely of Aboriginal people. He wanted to show the talent that he knew his family and people possessed, so along with his nephews, nieces and grannies was me. Well, I was a part of the family now.

We employed a few different white boys along the road for the minor role we needed until we reached Brisbane. There we found an Aboriginal boy who looked white enough. We dyed his hair red and had our own *wetjala nop* (white boy) for the east coast tour.

This is when I considered acting as an occupation.

Here I was, travelling around Australia, with all my expenses and airfares paid for. All I had to do was put in a couple of hours per night and enjoy the ride. I could handle this I thought, and started to relax.

I couldn't relax for long. In Sydney in October 1982 I really saw who Jack Davis the man was. There we were on the other side of Australia, a long way from home, and inside the Opera House: suddenly I was made aware of who I was. Lynette Narkle (who was also in his first production *Kullark*) delivered the monologue after the character played by Jack had died. I began to understand why I was there ...

Stark and white the hospital ward
In the morning sunlight gleaming,
But you are back in the moodgah now
Back on the path of your Dreaming.

I looked at him, then back through the years,
Then knew what I had to remember ...

And I knew, too, what I personally had to remember. Our old people were dying and their stories were dying with them. I needed my past in my future, and I realised we all needed to remember, before all that we had was reduced only to dreams:

I will let you dream - dream on old friend
Of a child and a man in September,
Of hills and stars and the river's bend;
Alas, that is all to remember.

When Lynette delivered her monologue, I would be lying on the couch on-stage and in semi-darkness watch a once proud man now reduced to just feeble words.

From then on I would watch Uncle Jack play his role night after night. This cheeky old man, who was full of spirit and laughter, tormented the audience and called them into his heart from where he spoke. It occurred to me that he wasn't acting. His portrayal was real. Jack was saying the very words he wanted to be heard.

I watched him from the wings. I watched him from on-stage and I watched the audience watch him. Every night they came in droves, black and white, and enjoyed his performance, like I did. Watching him before the performance, he was just J. D., laughing and carrying on like the rest of us, yet on-stage he was the spirit of every Aboriginal elder before him.

It was interesting being a member of an all-Aboriginal cast. I remember the stage manager and touring manager cursing the lack of professionalism we displayed in our approach to the 'rules of theatre'. We thought nothing of switching from being our larrikin selves, spinning yarns, teasing and joking even in the wings, to instantly becoming our characters with just one step on to the stage. We believed in what we were doing, we just did it in a different way. There was no thought to degrade our Aboriginality, our writers or ourselves.

Even on-stage Uncle Jack would break the rules.

Like when he had to wake, cough a heavy smoker's cough and spit (as his character was meant to do). We'd silently laugh. The audience always gasped in horror. I'd laugh at their reaction and think kindly of the old men of my past he epitomised. He was showing the reality of the aged men who lived with dirt floors in makeshift dwellings. Poverty is never pretty and death has never required social graces.

From *The Dreamers* I was convinced I wanted to pursue an acting career. I returned to Sydney seven months later with the words Uncle Jack had put into my head. 'You can do a lot neph.' That's all he said. That's all he needed to say. He went back to the pen. I knew we would meet again.

After nearly three years on the east coast I received a phone call from Andrew Ross asking about my availability for another of jack's plays. 'That Moonface bloke', Jack would call Andrew, and a few other choice names at times.

Andrew would always push Jack to write more of his emotions into the script. Jack lost sleep writing, Andrew lost hair trying to get him to write. They were compatible with each other and there was never a dull moment. Phone calls, late night visits, weekend houndings, Jack swearing, Andrew cursing and the result was *No Sugar*.

Kullark took us out of the city, back to the country.

The Dreamers took us out of Western Australia, and *No Sugar* was to take us overseas. With the addition of a few more relatives, the usual gang was again cast in this new play and 'to get it right', Jack was again an actor. His role of a tracker was not demanding, but was one from which he could watch the script and enjoy a holiday with us in Melbourne and Canada.

His role was also to provide the linking music, with the harmonica, between each scene from wherever he was on the stage, That was scary at times because you could never tell where he would turn up next, or even if he remembered to take along the harmonica. Richard Walley played his offsider and soon learnt to have a spare one and occasionally to use it.

We were also glad that it was not important to listen to a particular musical tune as the cue to the opening of the next scene. Jack would play what he felt like playing at the time, and there were numerous occasions when the older members in the audience would reminisce to that beautiful old tune that he played, but that they just couldn't remember the name of. Little did they know that the tune was something that Jack had just created from the mixture of the many tunes that meandered through his mind.

I along with other fortunate Aboriginal actors was lucky to be able to start in theatre with J. D. Lucky because we had no theatrical training to become actors, but his scripts were so close to our upbringing there was no need for training. We did it like we lived it. And we were proud to know that no theatre training school in Australia could teach us to act like the Aboriginals that he wanted us to be. Proud, upstanding and family. Together.

Lynette Narkle, John Moore, Kelton Pell, Dot Collard, Shane Abdulla, jedda Cole and Richard Walley are Aboriginal names that you hear about from the performing arts in Western Australia. Their base, like mine, is from his stables.

My moving to Sydney paid off with work in TV., films and stage productions. His advice - 'be yourself, if not, look for someone you know in your own family and play them' - is the best I have ever received. I have been doing that ever since. Thank you Uncle Jack. You know we will meet again.

'Spanning the Sky with Outstretched Hands': The Making of a Poet

DAVID HEADON

For over twenty years, white readers and literary critics have been struggling to develop strategies that might help them to understand Aboriginal literature. What exactly *is* good Aboriginal writing? What are its main themes? Directions? Priorities?" Particular strengths? Poet and social commentator Judith Wright stimulated the discussion in its earliest stages when, in 1973, she referred to the 'socioliterature of Aborigines'.[1] Could it be, Wright asked, that Aboriginal literature might' actually force non-Aboriginal readers to alter their standards of judgement, perhaps even modify their 'Western values and standards ... '?

In the years following Wright's essay, readers and critics struggled with its implicit challenges. John Beston quite inaccurately maintained that 'the work of the Aboriginal poets constitutes a sad literature'.[2] It does not. Aboriginal activist Bobbi Sykes categorically (and incorrectly) rejected the 'protest literature title that whites try and lay on black writers ... '[3] It wasn't until the early 1980s that greater insight into the nature of Aboriginal writing prevailed.

Bob Hodge, for example, built usefully on Wright's arguments. However, it was Aboriginal writer and critic Mudrooroo Narogin (then Colin Johnson) who put the most portentous stamp on the debate when he wrote in 1983:

> *Perhaps the most that can be said for modern Australian literature, or rather current literature, is its utter complacency and the fact that it is becoming more and more irrelevant to the society*

with which it seeks to deal. Aboriginal literature is and can be more
vital in that it is seeking to come to grips with and define a people,
the roots of whose culture extend in an unbroken line far back into a
past in which English is a recent intrusion.[4]

Aboriginal writers had begun to assert themselves;
Aboriginal writing could no longer be dismissed, ignored or
stereotyped. Kevin Gilbert, one of the most profound of the
Aboriginal writers, consolidated the unique (and
provocative) status of Aboriginal writing in white Australia's
bicentennial year when he introduced his *Inside Black
Australia* (1988) with the claim that the poems in his
anthology 'are not poems of protest, but rather, poems of life,
of reality.'[5] For Gilbert, Aboriginal poems are tough, direct
and uncompromising because Aboriginal life in Australia is,
too.

Jack Davis's four books of poems span twenty-two
years of Aboriginal social, political and cultural
development: *The First-born and Other Poems* (1970); *Jagardoo:
Poems from Aboriginal Australia* (1978); *John Pat and Other
Poems* (1988); and, most recently, *Black Life: Poems* (1992).[6]
Critical reception of these volumes was inevitably affected by
the fact that readers throughout the period grappled
nervously with the entire range of Aboriginal writing. Only
John Beston, Bob Hodge, Adam Shoemaker and Mudrooroo
Narogin have written anything at all substantial about the
verse of Jack Davis-and all four have, in different ways, been
side-tracked by issues which have affected their judgement.
The prevailing wisdom is that Davis's success as a dramatist
far outweighs his achievements as a poet. Beston, in the
mid-1970s, damned Davis's verse with faint praise when he
labelled him 'the gentlest and most contained' of the
Aboriginal poets.[7] Adam Shoemaker (1989) said there was
little 'uniquely Aboriginal' in the poems of either Davis or
Oodgeroo Noonuccal (Kath Walker);[8] Bob Hodge recently

maintained that, compared to his plays, Davis's 'poetry tends to be conventional in form and subject matter, and has not reached a wide audience';[9] while, in his *Writing from the Fringe* (1990), Mudrooroo was particularly severe, maintaining that Davis's poetry reveals him as a member of 'a generation scarred by assimilation' who therefore directs his verse 'at a European readership'. Mudrooroo goes further:

> *The aim is to destroy the type of poetry directed at the majority [white Australian] community by poets such as Jack Davis and Oodgeroo Noonuccal and to replace it with the desires ill the shape of language and structure which are found ill the depths of Aboriginal being.*

Ultimately, Mudrooroo labels the poetry of Davis and Noonuccal as 'invalid', as an 'active agent in suppressing any development of Aboriginal arts which lie outside this [Western] standard.[10]

If Jack Davis's powerful plays have been enthusiastically reviewed in recent years, clearly the same cannot be said for his poetry. Why is this? There appear to be several reasons. Firstly, it is true that his poetic technique owes much not to Aboriginality but to European traditions. Some oritics demand the reverse. In recent interviews; Davis has pointed to the fact that English is his first language ('My Aboriginal language is my second language'[11]). Jack grew up with a mother who specialised in making English meals such as Yorkshire pudding, while his early reading days were dominated by comic books, novels like *Huck Finn*, and the dictionary, He still embraces Christianity as a component of his spiritual beliefs and he acknowledges that 'the English poets were wonderful' in his formative years, especially Wordsworth, Keats and Shakespeare.[12] Secondly, Davis openly admits that he writes poetry that 'most people can understand ... because it's not really heavy stuff'.[13] Largely due to what he has called his 'fairly short' attention span, he aims at producing poems with 'a good finish, a good middle and a good start'.[14] Such deceptively simple aims don't impress readers/critics educated at white Australian middle-class universities that value aesthetic sophistication and intellectual density. Thirdly, by his own admission, Davis writes consciously aware of the fact that his majority audience will be white. Book sales are a factor. Reasonably enough, Davis wants as many people as possible to read what he has to say. He would not back away from the term 'popular poet', whereas the academy often does.

Many readers of Davis's poetry, both Aboriginal and white, have imposed their own rigid attitudes and views on his poetry. They have wanted him to write in a particular, politically correct way, wanting either more Aboriginal or more complex verse, or both. Davis has consistently ignored this pressure. He loves poems and poetry writing. Indeed, despite the enormous popularity of his plays, he has stated that poetry is 'a much happier medium' for him.[15] His poems are personal, passionate and, above all, a form of release. A therapy, if you like. As he puts it in the poem 'Let's Go':

> *I want to stand alone*
> *in a sea of words*
> *pluck out the phrases*
> *soar like a bird*
> *I want to stand on a mountain*
> *wait for the dawn*
> *yet be aware of*
> *the approach of a storm.*

While fully aware of the social and political responsibilities he has as a leader of his people, Davis demands artistic independence.

There is obviously a significant gap between Jack Davis's sense of his own poetry and the judgements of the majority of critics. Who is right? Let us put one of the most prominent critical assertions to the test: the claim that Davis is the. 'gentlest' of the Aboriginal poets, one of the more conventional versifiers. In fact, the opposite is true. In all four of his poetry volumes, Davis has maintained a robust, outspoken commitment to his people. His comment a couple of years ago that writing is 'the one thing which will bring change ... '[16] provides insight into the combative side of his nature. However, while Davis has always been a political poet, in the years from *First-born* to *Black Life* he has cleverly refined his poetic technique and strategies.

Kevin Gilbert was right when he said that with *First-born* 'Jack firmly established himself as an Aboriginal poet shouting, sobbing, demanding that his song, the Aboriginal song against injustice, be heard')? Several of his earliest poems are intentionally abrasive, alluding to the realities of life on the other side of the frontier. 'Laverton Incident', for example, anticipates the poems on black deaths in custody to follow in later books while 'Skeletal' takes up the issue (well before it was put on state government agendas) of Aboriginal remains illegally and immorally used for scientific purposes. Ritual killing, Aboriginal reserves and the excesses of European technology also inspire individual poems. But in his first book Davis is still searching for his poetic voice. 'The Painter' articulates the dilemma:

> *This is a canvas I can see:*
> *Death in the park and misery;*
> *The saddened face of a hungry child*
> *With matted hair and eyes half wild;*
> *An upraised hand, a blow on flesh,*
> *The curious sound of tortured breath.*

This scene so fills my mind and heart
I flex my fingers, tum to start;
But at the sound of one faint word
My colours run and all is blurred.

Both the tools and the subjects for protest remain elusive.

The political poems in *Jagardoo* (1978) are more assured and defiant than those in *First-born*. Mudrooroo maintains that they represent 'some of [Davis's] strongest pieces', and also that the set which includes 'Aboriginal Australia', 'Walker', 'Wrong or Right?' and 'Urban Aboriginal' contains numerous 'crisp and Aboriginal' images.[18] If one considers only Davis's first three volumes of verse, then this is true. 'Aboriginal Australia', in particular, bluntly presents the history of indigenous people in this country, both past and present, as it gathers the evidence of

a people crucified
The real Australian story.

However, it is worth noting that only about one-third of the poems in *Jagardoo* have an Aboriginal theme. The others reflect, as Judith Wright points out in her introduction to the volume, Davis's 'compassion, wisdom and humanity, and his experience of human tragedy.'[19] In poems such as 'Bombay', 'Flying from Nigeria' and 'The Affluent Society', Davis is representative of Western man. The epigraph to *Jagardoo* - 'To all who fight for freedom's sake' - takes on new meaning as we realise that the poet is beginning to widen his concerns to incorporate global questions.

The Aboriginal poems in *John Pat and Other Poems* (Davis's third volume, published in 1988 and dedicated to 'Maisie Pat, and to all mothers who have suffered similar loss') gain strength from Davis's increasing political and poetic assurance. As he said in an interview in 1981:

I really think the majority of Australians are just buffoons. They tell us to forgive and forget what's happened in the past. Then, every Anzac Day, they glorify their own history. How are we supposed to forget what's happened to us in Australia when white Australians keep on remembering their own violent history elsewhere? Besides, we have a lot more to remember right here. [20]

Davis makes certain that John Pat, a sixteen-year-old Aboriginal boy who died of head injuries after a disturbance between police and Aborigines in Roebourne (Western Australia) in 1983, will not be forgotten. Four police were charged with manslaughter and acquitted. 'John Pat' begins with haunting simplicity:

> *Write of life*
> *the pious said*
> *forget the past*
> *the past is dead.*
> *But all I see*
> *in front of me*
> *is a concrete floor*
> *a cell door*
> *and John Pat.*

These last three lines echo in a refrain through the poem-a poem which emerges as a stark prologue to Davis's play *Barungin (Smell the Wind)* (1989) where the last speaker, Meena, provides a grim catalogue of Aborigines who have died in custody in cells around the country.

Another powerful poem in *John Pat* is 'One Hundred and Fifty Years', written in protest at the exclusion of Aborigines from the white sesqui-centenary celebrations in Western Australia. This poem might well be taken as a companion piece to the earlier 'Aboriginal Australia' as it summarises a century and a half of incursions upon the local Aboriginal people. It is striking revisionist history, with the Western Australian pioneer icon, Captain Stirling, labelled as the 'first mass murderer' in the state. As in 'John Pat', a poignant stanza recurs:

> *So now that the banners have fluttered,*
> *the eulogies ended and the tattoos have rendered*
> *the rattle of spears,*
> *look back and remember the end of December*
> *and one hundred and fifty years.*

In her foreword to *Black Life: Poems* (1992), Oodgeroo stated that the volume is Davis's 'greatest' so far. She was right. At times the mature dramatist and poet merge to produce a book of courage and impressive breadth. The fact that only about ten poems are about Aborigines and the rest, as Davis has said, 'are just about life as I see it', works most effectively. Contrasts and correspondences dominate the eighty or so pages. Established themes are revisited, renewed: black deaths in custody ('Earth People', 'Cell Death' and' 'Move In'), the brutal reality of the colonial frontier ('Tapestry', 'The Land at the Brewery', 'A Letter to the Shade of Charles Darwin' and 'Rottnest'), contemporary Aboriginal life ('Black Life', 'The Fight to Save Bennett Brook') and the legacy of European invasion ('Remembering').

In *Black Life,* Jack Davis lays legitimate claim to being one of Australia's most challenging political poets. The voice, so assured when compared to the early poems, consoles, grieves, humiliates, attacks. The craft of poetry seems now to come more easily to poems such as the iconoclastic 'Earth People':

Blacks in South Africa are clumsy
they fall off balconies
out of windows
tumble down stairs
maybe they don't like tall buildings
They are earth people

Blacks in Australia
have strange habits also
Such as climbing up walls with singlet or sock ...
They too are earth people.

The analogy is acute, the indictment of two post-colonial societies a savage one. Continuity between the injustices of the present and past is established in 'The Land at the Brewery', which concludes:

They passed their laws
then drew a veil of death across
the children of the sun

- and also in 'A Letter to ... Darwin' as the speaker, 'Sylvester Squatter', mouths the platitudes of the arrogant, murderous invader:

we led them out of barbarism
into the era of Christendom by baptising
bibling blanketing and clothing them.

The omnipotent speaker in 'Remembering' condemns white society with measured accusations which have great impact because the poet resists diatribe:

They can forgive you
for the land you have stolen ...
the island prisons
the chain and the gun
But what they cannot forget is
you have slowed their heartbeat
and cast brute shadows
over the face of their sun.

Jack Davis is no gentle versifier. His published verse of the last two decades points to a poet who has worked hard at his craft both for love and for the political opportunities the genre can provide. However, several more observations can be made about his impressive output of poems: the pessimism of the early poems steadily evolves into a cautious optimism, or, at the very least, a resolve that Aboriginal people will continue to fight and survive; throughout his poetry, Davis retains a passionate belief in children and the redemptive qualities of youthful innocence; over the years, Davis has grown more acutely aware of the inherent value of nature and his own Aboriginal heritage; and, finally, in the poetry of *John Pat* and *Black Life*, he recognises and emphasises the importance of the shared global experience. As Davis says himself in *Aboriginal Writing Today* (1985): 'I just think I write for people.'[21]

First, the evolution from pessimism to guarded optimism. While, as Justine Saunders (1989) has observed, the message 'We have survived' runs through 'all of Jack Davis's work', it must be said that much of the verse in *First-born* is either backward-looking or deeply pessimistic.[22] In poems such as 'My Brother, My Sister', 'The Drifters' and 'The Red Gum and I', the speaker grieves for the earlier, pristine culture, pre-invasion, while in the title poem, along with 'Whither?' and 'Aboriginal Reserve', we are overwhelmed with the ravages of the present. The opening lines of the 'The Drifters' are typical:

> *We are the drifters, the faceless ones.*
> *Turn your heads as we walk by.*
> *we are the lost, forgotten sons,*
> *Bereft in a land of plenty.*
>
> *Where is the spear of days gone by?*

'The Red Gum and I' ends with a plaintive cry to 'Take us back where we belong'. The tone of these poems replicates Oodgeroo's (Kath Walker's) 'We Are Going'; the present is one of hopelessness and death. 'Whither?', possibly the best of the poems in the first volume, ends in utter despair:

> *So leave us now to continue our crying,*
> *There's nothing left for us now but the terror of dying.*

Jagardoo, as Kevin Gilbert has said, is (like *First-born*) another 'cry for justice',[23] but the tone of some of the poems in the second volume is different-at once more assertive and impatient, perhaps because of Davis's work as editor of the activist Aboriginal periodical *Identity* (1972-1979). Hope, survival and, above all, resilience and strength, are implicit in the last lines of 'Wrong or Right?':

> *I think you all can go to hell*
> *With your white-washed piety*

- and the last stanza of 'Urban Aboriginal':

> *With murder, with rape, you marred their skin,*
> *But you cannot whiten their mind;*
> *They will remain my children for ever,*
> *The black and the beautiful kind.*

This, no doubt, is an example of what Mudrooroo calls the 'sweet blackness'[24] in *Jagardoo*. The same quality pervades several of the poems in *John Pat* such as the dynamic 'Walk On', 'Dingo' and 'Boomer'. In the latter, poet and old-man kangaroo are one, united in the need to fight and survive:

> *He will fight for his mob,*
> *he's done it before,*
> *with sabre feet,*
> *and slashing claw.*
>
> *To their haven the hills*
> *they leap away,*
> *to live again*
> *for another day*

In an interview given just before his play *The Dreamers* opened in England as part of a programme marking the two-hundredth anniversary of the First Fleet, Davis defiantly announced: 'If we're celebrating anything, we're celebrating the survival of the Aboriginal people against all odds'.[25] This attitude is a far cry from the sentiments expressed in *First-born* and, as we might expect, it provides the fabric for most of the Aboriginal poems in *Black Life*.

The wonder, wisdom and innocence of childhood also figure prominently in numerous Davis poems. His memoirs and interviews reinforce the importance of his own fond memories in realising the superb quality of many of these childhood poems. Keith Chesson's *Jack Davis - A Life Story* (1988) and Davis's own *A Boy's Life* (1991) take up the story in detail,[26] but the introductory pages of *First-born* provide a useful autobiographical starting point as Davis recalls his idyllic early years in Yarloop, Western Australia. He was, as he says, 'always happy there'[27] in the period before his father's death, as we see in poems such as 'Retrospect' and

'The Boy and the Robin' (in *First-born*) and 'Cicada', 'Albert Barunga' and 'The Vine I' (in later books). 'Cicada' is my personal favourite, with its delicate, nostalgic images as the speaker (clearly Davis himself, rather than a persona figure) recalls:

> *a song of summer gold*
> *fading in the west,*
> *and a barefoot boy of twelve years old*
> *knowing home is best.*

It is almost certain that the cultural abundance of Jack Davis's childhood provided him with the catalyst for his discovery - or, more correctly, rediscovery - of the therapeutic value of nature and the crucial significance of his Aboriginal heritage. Both loom large, and are integrated with confidence and a sureness of touch in the later books *John Pat* and *Black Life*. However, in early poems such as 'The Aboriginal Stockman', 'Warru' and 'The Artist', along with the first bracket of eleven poems on nature in Jagardoo, the poet initially wrestles with the problem of finding the most appropriate creative strategies. These poem's are presumably the 'conventional' ones to which critics have referred. 'Day Flight' is a case in point. Here, the speaker/poet observes:

> *Far down below my country gleamed*
> *In thin dry rivers and blue-white lakes*
> *And most I longed for, there as I dreamed,*
> *A square of the desert, stark and red,*
> *To mould a pillow for a sleepy head*
> *And a cloak to cover me.*

The relationship between the speaker and the land below is essentially a passive one: distanced, remote. The land only protects; it does not inspire. 'Death of a Tree', in *Jagardoo*, is another example of a relatively early poem where the response to nature reflects the political and cultural uncertainty of the speaker.

The later books contain more generous, more satisfied responses. Ronald Berndt, in his preface to *Kullark* and *The Dreamers* written in 1982, suggests that 'Jack Davis's dream is of an Aboriginal heritage-not in terms of the past as such, but as a symbolic anchorage for the present ... '.[28] These comments seem particularly relevant to Davis's more recent verse. Poems like 'Black Cockatoos', 'Galahs', 'Soul', 'My Mother the Land', 'Summer Scene' and 'Raindrops' effortlessly establish a sense of the certainty in nature. 'Space Dreamer' and 'Land' (both in *John Pat*) celebrate the transcendental possibilities of this new relationship, the former poem beginning in ecstatic deference to the creative process itself:

> *Oh, I can span the sky with outstretched hands,*
> *I can leap through the curtains of nights,*
> *I can mirror the seas the winds the lands*
> *Within my fancied flights*

- while 'Land' concludes:

> *Her loveliness is summer red, pink fading gold,*
> *as mother sun sinks to fold*
> *herself in a cloak of night*
> *embossed with the light*
> *of stars from a black nation's dreamtime.*

Jack Davis, poet of the late 1980s, is a completely different proposition to the sometimes diffident, awkward writer of poems such as 'The Boomerang', 'Death of a Snake', 'Prejudice' and 'Maureen' twenty years earlier. A range of poems in *John Pat* and *Black Life* assert this new identity, among them 'Aboriginal Man', 'I Am', 'Three Generations', 'The Album' and 'Time'. 'I Am' is central:

My name is english
But I know my roots
my tribe my skin name
I am irrefutably indisputably
proudly Aboriginal.

The poem 'Time' is one of Davis's finest, as he aspires to the role of seer and prophet of his people. It ends:

If I could catch the drift
of tides
I then could
stand inside
the very heart beat of
my people's history.

In *Black Life*, Davis emerges as a vital pulse-beat of his people and his country. As that most profound of Australian critics Veronica Brady has said of him: ' ... the point of his writing is sharing, to speak for and with others who shared his experiences.'[29] Typically, his anti-nuclear poems (like 'Yellowcake', 'Nuclear', 'Mutation' and 'Iron Core') contain vital news for everyone, Aboriginal and non-Aboriginal alike.

Jack Davis is now in his mid-seventies and shows no sign of slowing down. His output over the last fifteen years has been prodigious; he writes as a driven man. And no wonder. Almost a third of all Aboriginal people in Australia today are homeless. Many endure Fourth World living conditions, suffering from diseases of poverty such as gastroenteritis, malnutrition, respiratory disease and tuberculosis. Confronted by these appalling facts, all Aboriginal writing has to be what Kevin Gilbert has called 'freedom writing.'[30] Davis's plays have been almost universally praised for their dramatic quality, innovation and socio-political commentary. His poems have not. Billy

Marshall-Stoneking wrote in 1983 that Davis is 'one of Australia's foremost original poets'. This claim, as I have suggested, was premature. However, on the basis of the poems in *John Pat* and *Black Life*, it can now be stated with confidence. Jack Davis's poetry is not a maintained that, compared to his plays, Davis's poetry tends to be conventional in form and subject matter, and has not modest appendix to his plays; it represents a corpus of work which demands attention in its own right. We all have something to learn from him.

Notes

1 Judith Wright, 'The Koori Voice: A New Literature', *Australian Author*. Vol. 5, No.4 (October 1973). p. 43.

2 John Beston, The Aboriginal Poets in English: Kath Walker, Jack Davis and Kevin Gilbert', *Meanjin*. Vol. 36, No.4 (December 1977). p.461.

3 Bobbi Sykes. quoted in Adam Shoemaker. *Black Words. White Page: Aboriginal Literature 1929-1988.* University of Queensland Press. St Lucia. Qld. 1989. p. 189.

4 Colin Johnson [Mudrooroo Narogin]. 'White Forms. Aboriginal Content'. *Aboriginal Writing Today.* ed. Jack Davis and Bob Hodge. Australian Institute of Aboriginal Studies. Canberra, ACT. 1985. p. 28.

5 Kevin Gilbert, ed. *Inside Black Australia: An Anthology of Aboriginal Literature*. Penguin. Melbourne. Vic. 1988. p. xxiv.

6 All quotations from the poetry of Jack Davis used in this article can be found in the following: *The First-born and Other Poems.* Angus and Robertson. Sydney. NSW. 1970; *Jagardoo: Poems from Aboriginal Australia,* Methuen. Sydney. NSW. 1978; *John Pat and Other Poems,* Dent. Melbourne. Vic. 1988; *Black Life: Poems.* University of Queensland Press. St Lucia. Qld, 1992.

7 Beston, p. 461.

8 Shoemaker. p. 192.

9 Bob Hodge and Vijay Mishra, ed. *Dark Side of the Dream: Australian Literature and the Postcolonial Mind.* Allen & Unwin, Sydney. NSW. 1991. p. 108.

10 Mudrooroo Narogin. *Writing fram the Fringe: A Study of Modern Aboriginal Literature,* Hyland House. Melbourne. Vic. 1990. pp. 38-49.

11 Gerry Turcotte. ed. *Writers in Action: The Writer's Choice Evenings.* Currency Press. Sydney. NSW. 1990. p. 191.

12 Turcotte. p. 20 I; *First-born.* p. ix; Turcotte. p. 189.

13 Turcotte, p. 200.

14 Turcotte, p. 201.

15 Liz Thompson, comp., *Aboriginal Voices: Contemporary Aboriginal Artists, Writers and Performers*, Simon & Schuster, Brookvale, NSW, 1990, p. 16.

16 Turcotte, p. I 82. 17 Gilbert, p. 53.

18 Narogin, pp. 82-4.

19 Jagardoo, p. viii.

20 Shoemaker, p. 128.

21 Davis and Hodge, p. 19.

22 Justine Saunders in *Plays from Black Australia: Jack Davis, Eva Johnson, Richard Walley, Bob Maza*, Currency Press, Sydney, NSW, 1989, p. viii.

23 Gilbert, p. 53.

24 Narogin, p. 82.

25 David Britton, 'Drag on bicentennial of brutality', *Canberra Times*, Sunday, May 24 (1987).

26 Keith Chesson, *Jack Davis - A Life Story*, Dent, Melbourne, Vic, 1988; *Jack Davis, A Boy's Life*, Magabala Books, Broome, W.A., 1991.

27 *First-born*, p. xiii.

28 Jack Davis, *Kullark/The Dreamers*, Currency Press, Sydney, NSW, 1982,p.xxi.

29 Veronica Brady, 'The Environment: *A Bran Nue Dae* or a Very Ancient One?', *Westerly*, Vol. 36, No.4 (December 1991), p. 102.

30 Brady, p. 101.

STUDY QUESTIONS

1.   What is the function of the actors' break from character in Act Two, Scene One and Act Two, Scene Five of *Kullark*?

2.   What effect does humour have in Davis's plays?

3.   Construct as many different 'times' as you can for *Kullark* and/or *Barungin*. How many of these are found in white history books? Why are some of them not found in white history books?

4.   What purpose does the trivial pursuit game III *Barungin* serve?

5.   Examine the Dreamer figure in *The Dreamers* and Yagan in *Kullark*. How do they express the Aboriginal understanding of history? How is that understanding connected to the oral tradition?

6.   How would you stage the corroboree in *No Sugar*?

7.   Davis says that Aborigines are always forced to act in the white world. How does this relate to the plays?

8.   What was it like to be Aboriginal in Australia in the late 1960s? Is it any different today? Why?

9.   In what ways have social, cultural and political developments in Australia over the last twenty years affected Jack Davis's poetry?

10.   Discuss any five Davis poems as works of history.

11.   Discuss Davis's 'Christian' poems as a reflection of his spiritual beliefs.

12.   Discuss Davis's poems on childhood as a reflection of his personal philosophy of life.

13.   How does the issue of black deaths in custody impact on the poetry of Jack Davis?

14.   How important is nature in the poetry of Davis?

15.   How important is Davis's Aboriginal heritage to him? Choose one poem from each of his books as a starting point.

16.   Jack Davis's poetry deals with the reality of 'the other side of the frontier' and the facts of Western Australian history. Discuss any five poems which address the 'frontier' theme.

17.   Is Jack Davis a political poet? Is this description too restricting?

18.   Act out a scene from one of Davis's plays paying particular attention to the 'space' in which the drama is performed. How can space itself be part of the message of the play?

Select Bibliography
Primary Bibliography

Davis, Jack, *A Boy's Life*, Magabala Books, Broome, WA,1991.

Davis, Jack, 'Aboriginal Writers', in *Identity*, VoL 3, No.8 (October 1978), pp. 16-17.

Davis, Jack, *Barungin (Smell the Wind)*, Currency Press, Sydney, NSW, 1989.

Davis, Jack, 'Barungin (Smell the Wind)', in *Writers in Action: The Writer's Choice Evenings*, ed, Gerry Turcotte, Currency Press, Sydney, NSW, 1990, pp. 179-202.

Davis, Jack, *Black Life: Poems*, University of Queensland Press, St Lucia, Qld, 1992.

Davis, Jack, 'Growing Up in the Bush: A Recollection', in *Gone Bush*, ed. Roger McDonald, Bantam, Moorebank, NSW, 1990, pp. 147-60.

Davis, Jack, *Honey Spot*, illus, by Ellen Jose, Currency Press, Sydney, NSW, 1987.

Davis, Jack, *In Our Town*, Currency Press, Sydney, NSW,1992.

Davis, Jack, *Jack Davis* [video-recording], Audio-Visual Education Branch, Education Department of Western Australia, Perth, WA, 1982.

Davis, Jack, 'Jack Davis: Playwright and Poet', in *Aboriginal Voices: Contemporary Aboriginal Artists, Writers and Performers*, comp, Liz Thompson, Simon & Schuster, Brookvale, NSW, 1990, pp. 12-17.

Davis, Jack, *Jagardoo: Poems from Aboriginal Australia*, illus. by Harold Thomas,Methuen, Sydney, NSW, 1977.

Davis, Jack, *John Pat and Other Poems*, Dent, Ferntree Gully, Vic, 1988.

Davis, Jack, *Kullark/The Dreamers*, Currency Press, Sydney, NSW, 1982.

Davis, Jack, *Moorli and the Leprechaun.* Currency Press, Sydney, NSW, 1994.

Davis, Jack, *No Sugar*, Currency Press, Sydney, NSW, 1986.

Davis, Jack, 'The Dreamers', *Meanjin*, Vol. 43, No.1 (March 1984), pp. 45-48.

Davis, Jack, *The First-born and Other Poems*, Dent, Melbourne, Vic, 1983.

Davis, Jack, *Wahngin Country.* First performed in Perth, W A, 1992.

Davis, Jack, and Bob Hodge, ed.,
Aboriginal Writing Today (Papers
from the First National Conference
of Aboriginal Writers, held at
Murdoch University February
1983), Australian Institute of
Aboriginal Studies, Canberra, ACT,
1985.
Davis, Jack, Stephen Muecke,
Mudrooroo Narogin and Adam
Shoemaker, ed., *Paperbark: A
Collection of Black Australian
Writings*, University of Queensland
Press, St Lucia, Qld, 1990.

Secondary Bibliography

Balme, Christopher B., 'The Aboriginal Theatre of Jack Davis: Prolegomena to a Theory of Syncretic Theatre', in *Crisis and Creativity in the New Literatures in English: Cross/Cultures*, ed. Geoffrey V. Davis and Hena Maes-Jelinek, Rodopi, Amsterdam, 1990, pp. 401-17. Banks, Ron, 'A Lesson in Irony from the City's Back Door', *The West Australian*, 13 February 1992, p. 48. Banks, Ron, 'The Dreamers a First for Radio', *The West Australian*, 14 November 1990, p. 51.

Beach, Michael, 'Jack Davis Smells the Winds of Change', *The Australian Weekend Magazine*, 23-24 January 1988, p.2.

Bennett, Bruce, 'Writing West', *Westerly*, Vol. 31, No.1 (March 1986), p. 96.

Beston, John B., 'The Aboriginal Poets in English: Kath Walker, Jack Davis, and Kevin Gilbert', Meanjin, Vol. 36, No. 4 (December 1977), pp. 446-61.

Brady, Veronica, 'A Postmodernist City', *First Rights: a Decade of Island Magazil1e*, ed. Andrew San!: and Michael Denholm, Greenhouse Publications, Elwood, Vic, 1989, pp. 18-27.

Brady, Veronica, 'The Environment: *A Bran Nue Dae* or a Very Ancient One?', Westerly, Vol. 36, No.4 (December 1991), pp. 100-06.

Campbell, Lance, 'Dealing With the "White Problem"', *The Advertiser Magazine*, 27 February 1988, p. 5.

Cato, Nancy, 'An Australian Voice is Heard in Canada', *This Australia*, Vol. 6, No.1 (Summer 1987), pp. 88-89.

Chesson, Keith, *Jack Davis - A Life Story*, Dent, Melbourne, Vic, 1988.

Dashfield, Prue, 'Jack Davis: The Bridge Between Black and White', *The West Australian Magazine*, 1 September 1990, pp. 12-13 and pp. 15-16.

Devine, Frank, 'Currency Lads and Lasses Set the Stage for a National Theatre', *The Australian*, 9 September 1991, p.11.

Dibble, Brian, and Margaret MacIntyre, 'Hybridity in Jack Davis's No Sugar', *Westerly*, Vol. 37, No.4 (Summer 1992), pp.93-98.

Dunstone, Bill, 'Four New Plays', *Westerly*, Vol. 27, No.2 (June 1982), pp. 63-66.

Elder, Arlene A., 'Self, Other, and Post-Historical Identity in Three Plays by Jack Davis', *The Journal of Commonwealth Literature*, Vol. 25, No.1 (1990), pp. 204-15.

Evans, Bob, 'Jack Davis Smells Change on the Wind', *The Sydney Morning Herald*, 20 February 1988, p. 74.

Farmer, Alison, 'Chapter and Verse on Life from a Perth Park Bench', *The Weekend Australian*, 30 November-1 December 1991, Rev. 9.

Fitzpatrick, Peter, 'Mythmaking in Modern Drama', in *The Penguin New Literary History of Australia*, ed. Laurie Hergenhan, Penguin, Melbourne, Vic, 1988, pp.520-34.

Gilbert, Helen, 'Historical Re-Presentation: Performance and Counter-discourse in Jack Davis's Drama', *New Literatures Review*, No. 19 (Summer 1990), pp. 91-101.

Gilbert, Helen, 'The Dance as Text in Contemporary Australian Drama: Movement and Resistance Politics', Ariel, Vol. 23, No.1 (January 1.992), pp.133-47.

Gilbert, Kevin, ed., lnside Black Australia: All Allthology of Aborigillal Literature, Penguin, Melbourne, Vic, 1988.

Gillam, Cliff, 'Hesperian Varieties: New Western Australia Drama at the 1988 Festival of Perth', *Westerly*, Vol. 33, No. 2(June 1988), pp. 127-34

Graham, Duncan, 'Davis Spreads the Words', *The Age Saturday Extra*, 13 February 1988, p. 10.

Graham, Duncan, 'How the Black Swan was Hatched', *The Age Saturday Extra*, 24 August 1991, p. 8.

Graham, Duncan, 'Verse from the Inside', *The Age Saturday Extra*, 9 December 1989, p. 8.

Harley,]. B., 'Maps, Knowledge and Power', *The Icollography of Landscape*, ed. D. Cosgrove and S. Daniels, Cambridge University Press, Cambridge, 1988, pp. 277-312.

Harris, Michael, 'The Aboriginal Voice in Australian Poetry', *Antipodes*, Vol. 4, No.1 (Spring 1990), pp. 4-8.

Hodge, Bob and Vijay C. Mishra, ed., *Dark Side of the Dream: Australian Literature and the Postcolonial Mind*, Allen & Unwin, Sydney, NSW, 1991.

Indyk, Ivor, 'The Past in Present Writing', in *Memory*, ed. Ivor Indyk and Elizabeth Webby, Collins/Angus & Robertson, North Rvde, NSW, 1991, pp. 238-51.

Kerr, David, 'Fictionalising History: Problem and Promise in Black Literature', *Journal of Australian Literature*, Vol. 1, No.1 (June 1990), pp. 1-14.

Knudsen, Eva Rask, 'Fringe Finds Focus: Developments and Strategies in Aboriginal Writing in English', in European Perspectives: Contemporary Essays on Australian Literature (*Australian Literary Studies*, Vol. 15, No.2, 1991), ed. Giovanna Capone, Bruce Clunies-Ross and Werner Senn, University of Queensland Press, St Lucia, Qld, 1991,pp. 32-44.

Kraine-jones, Karen, 'Contemporary Aboriginal Drama', *Southerly*, Vol. 48, No. 4 (December 1988), pp. 432--44.

Langsam, David, 'Jack Davis and Marli Biyol in London', *Australian Society* (August 1988), pp. 41--42.

Laurie, Victoria, 'Black Stars Risen in the West', *The Bulletin*, Vol. 113, No. 5807 (18 February 1992), pp. 90-91.

Lewis, Berwyn, 'Smelling the Winds of Injustice', *The Weekend Australian*, 26-27 November 1988, p. 7.

McCallum, John, 'New Voices Unheard in a Dramatic Tragedy', *The Weekend Australian*, 20-21 June 1992, Rev. 11.

McPhee, Alex, *First-born: the Life and Times of Jack Davis* [video-recording], Zest films, in association with BBC Bookmark, 1988.

Milne, Geoffrey, 'Black and White in Australian Drama: Melbourne 1988', *Meridian*, Vol. 9, No.1 (May 1990), pp.33--43.

Milne, Geoffrey, '"Our Side of the Story": Plays from Black Australia', *Meridian*, Vol. 10, No.1 (May 1991), pp. 64-69

Narogin, Mudrooroo, 'A Short History of Aboriginal Writing', *The Independent Monthly*, Vol. 2, No.2 (August 1990), pp.36-38.

Narogin, Mudrooroo, *Writing from the Fringe: A Study of Modern Aboriginal Literature*, Hyland House, Melbourne, Vic, 1990. Now with ETT Imprint.

Nelson, Emmanuel S., 'Black America and the Australian Aboriginal Literary Consciousness', *Westerly*, Vol. 30, No.4 (December 1985), pp.43-54.

Nelson, Emmanuel S., ed., *Connections - Essays on Black Literatures*, Aboriginal Studies Press, Canberra, ACT, 1988.

Riemenschneider, Dieter, 'Australian Aboriginal Writing in English: the Short Story', *Antipodes*, Vol. 4, No.1 (Spring 1990), pp. 39-45. [Discusses two short stories, 'The Stone' and 'Pay Back'.]

Saunders, Justine, intro., *Plays from Black Australia: Jack Davis, Eva Johnson, Richard Walley, Bob Maza*, Currency Press, Sydney, NSW, 1989.

Schwartz, Larry, 'Face to Face: Political Acts', *The Good Weekend*, 7 May 1988, p. 9.

Scott, Maurie, 'Karbarra: The New Aboriginal Drama and its Audience', *Span*, No. 30 (April 1990), pp. 127-40.

Shoemaker, Adam, 'Aboriginal Play not for ACT', *The Canberra Times*, 17 October 1983, p. 12.

Shoemaker, Adam, 'Ari Interview with Jack Davis', *Westerly,* Vol. 27, No.4 (December 1982), pp. 111-16.

Shoemaker, Adam, *Black Words, White Page: Aboriginal Literature 1929-1988,* University of Queensland Press, St Lucia, Qld, 1989.

Shoemaker, Adam, 'Crossing at the Intersection: Native Australian and Canadian Writing', *Meridian,* Vol. 11, No.1 (May 1992), pp.4-13.

Shoemaker, Adam, '"Fiction or Assumed Fiction": The Short Stories of Colin Johnson, Jack Davis, and Archie Weller', in *Connections: Essays on Black Literatures,* ed. & introd. Emmanuel S. Nelson, Aboriginal Studies Press, Canberra, ACT, 1988, pp.53-59.

Shoemaker, Adam, and Jack Davis, 'Aboriginal Literature', in *The Penguin New Literary History of Australia,* ed. Laurie Hergenhan, Penguin, Melbourne, Vic, 1988, pp.27-46.

Simmonds, Diana, 'Jack's All Right', *The Bulletin,* Vol. 112, No. 5746 (20 November 1990), p. 27.

Simmonds, Diana, 'New and Notable', *The Bulletin,* Vol. 112, No. 5746 (20 November 1990), p. 152.

Strauss, Dagmar, *Facing Writers,* ABC Enterprises, Crows Nest, NSW, 1990, pp. 37-50.

Tapping, Craig, 'Oral Cultures and the Empire of Literature', *Kunapipi,* Vol. 11, No.1 (1989), pp. 86-96.

Tompkins, Joanne, 'Time Passed/Time Past: The Empowerment of Women and Blacks in Australian Feminist and Aboriginal Drama', *Australasian Drama Studies,* No. 19 (October 1991), pp.13-22.

Turcotte, Gerry, '"Recording the Cries of the People": An Interview with Oodgeroo Noonuccal', *Aboriginal Culture Today,* ed. Anna Rutherford, Dangaroo Press, Sydney, NSW, 1988, pp. 16-30.

Turcotte, Gerry, ed., *Writers in Action: The Writer's Choice Evenings,* Currency Press, Sydney, NSW, 1990, pp. 179-202.

Usher, Rod, 'Shelf Life', *The Age Saturday Extra,* 19 March 1988, p. 11.

Watego, Cliff, 'Backgrounds to . Aboriginal Literature', in *Connections: Essays on Black Literatures,* ed. & introd. Emmanuel S. Nelson, Aboriginal Studies Press, Canberra, ACT, 1988, pp. 11-23.

Watts, Edward, 'In Your Head You are Not Defeated: the Irish in Aboriginal Literature', *The Journal of Commonwealth Literature,* Vol. 26, No.1· (1991), pp. 33-48.

Wright, Judith, 'The Koori Voice: A New Literature', *Australian Author,* Vol. 5, No.4 (October 1973), pp.38-44.

Notes on Contributors

Ernie Dingo is one of Australia's leading actors and comedians. He has starred in numerous television programs, plays and films including *Crocodile Dundee 2*, *The Fringe Dwellers* and *Bran Nu Dae*. In 1988 he won an AFI Best Actor Award for *A Waltz Through the Hills*, and in 1990 was awarded The Medal of Australia for services to the arts. He presented the program *The Great Outdoors* for 16 years.

Helen Gilbert lectures at the University of Quensland and is co-author (with J. Lo) of *Performance and Cosmopolitics: Cross-Cultural Transactions in Australia* (2007).

David Headon is a Senior Lecturer at the Australian National University. His edited or co-edited works include *Looking Beyond Yesterday: The Australian Artist and New Paths to Our Future* (1990), *North of the Ten Commandments: A Collection of Northern Territory Literature* (1991), *Crown or Country: The Traditions of Australian Republicanism* (1994), *Eureka— Australia's Greatest Story* (2015) and *Alfred Deakin—The Lives, the Legacy* (2018).

Oodgeroo Noonuccal (Kath Walker) was one of Australia's most celebrated writers and critics. Born on Stradbroke Island in 1920, she grew up on the shores of Mornington Bay, and was known to her people as Quandamooka. She wrote numerous books, including the best-selling *We Are Going* in 1964 and *Stradbroke Dreamtime* in 1972. She died in September 1993, aged 72.

Joanne Tompkins is a Professor at the University of Queensland. Her main research area is post-colonial drama, and her recent books include *Theatre's Heterotopias: Space and the Analysis of Performance (2014)* and *Unsettling Space: Contestations in Contemporary Australian Theatre* (2006); both Palgrave/Macmillan.

Adam Shoemaker is the Vice-Chancellor of Victoria University. He is the author of the award-winning study *Black Words, White Page*, is co-editor of the first national anthology of *Black Australian Writing, Paperbark,* and wrote *Mudrooroo: A Critical Study* (A & R). His later books include *Aboriginal Australians: First Nations of an Ancient Continent,* (with Stephen Muecke) Thames and Hudson.

Gerry Turcotte edited this volume. He is the author and editor of 18 books including the novel *Flying in Silence* which was shortlisted for *The Age* Book of the Year in 2001 and *Border Crossings: Words & Images* (both Brandl & Schlesinger). His newest book, *The Ghost Wilderness and Other Plays* was published in December 2021. He is President & Principal, of St Mark's College & Corpus Christi College, in Vancouver.

EDITOR'S NOTE

Jack Davis's plays and volumes of poetry have been· reprinted frequently and so there are occasionally variances between the editions cited by the respective authors and those in the bibliography. This is merely a reflection of the different editions used by the respective authors.

Printed in Australia
Ingram Content Group Australia Pty Ltd
AUHW021023250823
382752AU00005B/17